Kaleidoscope

Kaleidoscope
Collected Poems

Barbara Findley Stuart

Copyright © 2022 by Barbara Findley Stuart
All Rights Reserved
Manufactured in the United States of America

Cover and Book Design by the Publications Unit, Department of English, Illinois State University, Director: Steve Halle, Production Assistants: Saima Afreen and Emily Fontenot, Production Intern: Kamryn Freund

ISBN 979-8-218-07144-8

First Edition

Table of Contents

Zero Cold | 1
Flower Angel | 3
The Lovely Dark | 5
The House across the Street | 8
Dark Road | 10
Class Reunion | 12
University Degree | 15
Pioneer | 18
A Teacher Retires | 22
To My Brother, William Findley | 25
Journeys beyond Walls | 26
Jim | 29
Rose Branches | 31
The Almond Tree | 32
Time | 34
Easter Spring | 37
Love without Walls | 39
Three Gifts | 42
War and Peace | 44
Wedding Gift | 47
Return | 49
Small Bully | 51
The Pea-Pickin' Song | 53
Peeps Bunnies | 54
Addiction | 56

You Are What You Eat, or Miracle Cure! | 59
Cookie Jar | 61
To Hold My Hand: My Mom | 65
No Complaints | 69
A Pair of Stockings | 75
How Clever | 78
Words | 79
The Sculptured Poem | 82
The Path Ahead | 84
Passageways | 86
Lion out of Bounds | 87
Red Balloon | 89
Fireworks | 93
9-11: New York | 95
9-11: Pennsylvania | 96
Killing George Floyd | 99
Anger is a Frightened Horse | 104
Traffic Ticket | 105
Travel | 107
D-Day at Omaha Beach | 110
A Winter's Tale | 114
A Prayer for Our Government | 116
Puppeteer; 2017 | 118
Right the Third Time | 120
Merlin Kennedy | 124
The Paul Findley Trail | 127
John Lewis, Civil Rights Leader | 128
Ceremonies | 131

Young Black Man | 134
Impeachment Manager | 139
The Lawn | 141
Pandemic | 143
Fighting the Coronavirus | 146
Pandemic List | 150
The Plum Tree in Spring | 153
Time to Get Up | 154
Summertime Cat | 155
A Kitten's Tail | 157
If You Should Smile | 159
Difficult Doors | 160
Hidden Fire | 161
Fourth of July Fears | 164
Halloween Courage | 167
In Your Beginning | 170
Forgiving Dylann Roof | 172
Sometimes | 175
Memorial | 177
Knowing Their Name | 180
Christmas Morning | 182
November Leaves | 185
Amnesia | 186
Nosebleeds | 189
Hearing Aid Rescue | 193
Homecoming | 195
Shared Happiness | 198
In Touch | 201

Night Rain | 204
Morning Light | 206
Crystal Moment | 208
Old Hands | 211
Suncatcher | 214
Becoming Deaf | 216
November Light | 220
Cool Moon | 222
Transformation | 223
Epiphany | 225
Slam-Dunk | 226
Gifts of the Earth | 227
Creation | 231
Outer Space: Small Magellanic Cloud | 235
Autumn 1955 | 237
Queen of Trees | 239
A Mystery | 240
Sweetgum | 243
The Pin Oak in Winter | 246
Christmas Lights | 249
Colors of the Sun | 251

About the Author | 257

Kaleidoscope

My frosted window

Zero Cold

In zero cold
the sunshine
flashes diamond sparks from
my frost-encrusted
windowpanes—
an emperor's gallery
of icy masterworks,
lucent tapestries
of frost-leaves,
ice-etched snowflakes,
and sparkling
fantasy-flowers
ablaze in my sunny windows,
my wintry
crystal palace.

But in zero cold
those who have no home
and no frosted windows
die stiff
under bridges,
slowly frozen
in zero snow
that crunches under foot.

How beautiful,
yet how terrible,

this arctic wedding
of opposites—
forcing us to see our need
to learn from zero cold,
to search out warmth
and love
and wisdom
here upon
our frozen star.

                                    January, 2016

Flower Angel

It is dark, long past midnight.
Outside, an ice storm
has weighed down the trees
and an inches-thick coat of snow
has bowed them almost to the ground—
a white fantasy
from another world.

The glow from the snow
and the moon-lit clouds
floods through the hospital windows
making my room light as if it is dawn,
light enough for me to see
the flowers sent by my daughter
from far-away Texas
but not light enough to see
the pink, yellow, orange—
too dark for colors.

Strangely,
almost black against the white wall,
the greenery and flowers
have taken on the shape of an angel
standing there with outspread arms
kind, benevolent, patient,
with drooping sleeves,
and, mysteriously,

one 'hand' raised
in blessing.

Miserable and unable to sleep,
I need the angel's blessing.
And in the dimly lit silence
she brings me peace—
the peace
born of love.

January 2, 2021

The Lovely Dark

I can't sleep.
Nothing new about that!
Most nights
for two or three hours
I can't sleep.

So I try gimmicks.
Just now I am sick of lying still
counting deep breaths.
So I am wandering in the dark,
just wandering.

The house is silent.
I reach out
to turn on the hall light
and then flip it off,
watching its fluorescent spiral
glow a while longer,
mysterious in the sudden dark
—a small, quirky ghost.

Ahead, a tiny light
eyes me
from my neighbor's window
across the street
—a miniature beacon
reaching out to me

here in my dark hall.
God perhaps, I think,
sending a star
to keep me company.

I watch my little star
in the dark silence.
Peace engulfs me;
sleep no longer matters;
I am at last
calm
in the lovely dark.

March, 2015

Broadway in Normal, Illinois: Deep Snow

The House across the Street

*There it is, the house across the street.
I've seen it every day.*

*But covered with snow
backed by rosy clouds piled high
with black-fingered trees
silhouetted against the pinkish glow,
it's a picture from a magazine
or a coffee-table book—
and a house I've not seen before.*

But of course, after all, it's the same house
made new by the deep snow.
Underneath, the house is real
and has not changed.

What then is real and lasting?
Does everything change?
Or is there perhaps a spirit inside—
a soul—
something that does not change?
Does everything—the house, the snow
the neighbors—and I too—
share in some mysterious way
an essence that does not vanish?
Deep down I know that
there is a center within each of us,

a soul that, although it is always
changing,
will not vanish.

And I know that somewhere, somehow,
at the very center of everything,
of even the universe,
there is a luminous, loving,
enveloping presence
that does not change
and will never vanish.

January, 2008

Dark Road

Peering at me
from over the hill ahead,
two shafts of blinding light
pierce the silvery rain,
stare into my eyes,
and flash past,
leaving me once more
driving solitary into the dark.

My wiper blades
click a lonely syncopation
to the drumming of the rain.

A feckless firefly
mashes a yellow smear
across my windshield,
the stain wiping slowly away,
pale
against my bright fan of light
as I thrust through
the darkness ahead.

Three militant trees
rise out of the dark
and catch light-rings
from the glassy road,
slipping them up

their rain-darkened trunks
one at a time.

A black house
with gleaming windows
blinks past,
sheltering people within;
sheltering them
from the dark,
the rain,
the lonely road.

                    1957; revised 2019

Class Reunion
Princeton Township High School, Class of 1946

Yes, I know it is you
and I know it is me
that's underneath the wrinkles and gray hair.
    (Alternate words, choose—
    face lift and dyed hair)

I suppose you're getting deaf
and a little bit blind.
    MY eyesight AND my hearing are just fine.
    (What—?
    What's that you said?)

I don't mind getting old
since I know you are, too,
    (though God knows all these ailments are a pain)
but I do hate to say
though it's obviously true,
    I DO NOT show my age as much as you.
    (Just…help me up out of this chair…
    Would you?)

Now they say you are rich—
CEO at a bank!
    I tell you not from envy, nor to brag—
but I'm top dog at Mayo's
and my son advises Bush…
    So sorry you can't measure up to that…

(You'll pay the tip?　Well…
　　　If you INSIST!)

My whole life's been a dream.
Just one long sip of cream…
　　You're telling me you don't believe a WORD?
Well…a word… here and there…??
Oh.　　　OK.　　　But NO FAIR!
　　This may be my only chance to fake it!
　　　(We're all in this together!)

THREE CHEERS FOR THE CLASS OF '46!
GO!　FIGHT!　WIN!

　　　　　　1991

Grandson Zachary graduation, North Texas University Arena

University Degree

You are now an atom
in the sea of unisex/unicolor
mortarboards and gowns
that seethes and stirs and murmurs
before us.

You are surrounded
by a protective,
possessive
embankment of noisy families
vibrating with pride
and electric excitement,
Here she comes!
There he is! See?—in the 3rd row!

You are surrounded
by our love,
our immersion in your joy,
knowing your struggles—
but also unfortunately perhaps,
surrounded by parental pride:
My child
the university graduate!
and parental pressure,
Be successful!
You emerge now
from your sea of unifirmity

a starkly individual,
fingerling adult,
to seize your brief
joyous moment of glory.

It is a moment of symbolic honor
formally conferred upon you

by the well-paid
university president
in person.

In reality, it is
your moment of rebirth,
when you are popped out,
Free at last!
into what we call the real world
—only to confront a seascape
of new challenges.

Can I pay off my college debts?
Can I support a family?
Can I fulfill a meaningful purpose
with my life?

And the answer lies
in your hands
—the well-earned solid evidence
of your worth,
your shining degree—

a strong assist
as you face the world.

As you venture
we hope you will often say
to yourself,
I have found this
that I learned at the university
to be a treasure.
I intend to use it well
and pass it on
to others.

June 1, 2014

My Great-Grandmother, the doctor, at
100 years

Pioneer

Dr. Abigail Almira Kidder Nichols (1815–1917)

Death was a frequent guest
in Braintree, Vermont,
in the 1830s—
deaths of mothers
little children
tiny newborn babies;
deaths from measles and typhoid;
deaths from the dread smallpox.

So when Abigail read about
Florence Nightingale's
daring venture that made nursing

into important work for women—
not just for men—
she wanted to be a nurse.

Her prosperous
lawyer and legislator father said,
"No."
But she stood firm
and became a nurse
anyway.

She fell in love with
a handsome, kind preacher's son
with no money.
Her father again said
"No."
But she stood tall by Theodore
and became his wife
anyway.

They planned to go West.
Her father still said,
"No."

But they bought a covered wagon
anyway
and traveled with friends
through the Erie Canal
and on past Chicago—
"Way too swampy

to have a future!"
they said—
and they settled in Dover, Illinois
on a stretch of prairie
in the midst of woods and wolves
and Indians.

Soon Abigail found herself weeping
over her two sweet babies,
who died of cholera.
But then she and Theodore had
two daughters and three sons
who lived to old age.
And she ran a millinery shop
and played her piano
and taught school in a log cabin.
And she was a suffragette
for women's vote
and she was a prairie nurse!

She was busy.

But she began to feel that
being a nurse was not enough
—too many deaths
of little children and their mothers.
She wanted to be a doctor.
But doctors could only be men.

Her husband said, "I'll help you."

So she followed a doctor
on horseback visiting the sick,
doggedly enduring
blistering sun and icy winds.
She studied heavy textbooks
and passed examinations
and she became a certified doctor
—the first woman doctor
in the state of Illinois!

Now she would usher
hundreds of healthy babies
into prairie families—in safety.
She would care for
twenty typhoid patients
during the great epidemic
    and see them all live!
She felt honored;
she felt proud
to save so many lives.

She lived to be a hundred and two,
still reminding her grown children,
"Get enough sleep and eat right,"
and she rode her horse to church
until she was a hundred.

She was a pioneer.

                            June, 2019

A Teacher Retires

Teaching school has one thing
that ordinary life does not offer—
school comes to a halt, regularly,
to tally progress.

Teachers do this
with the regularity
of inch-marks on a ruler,
      lesson after lesson,
semester after semester,
marking these endings
with tests, grades, reports
—a clock chiming the hour.

And they say to themselves each time,
Did I do all I should have?
Did I do it well?
Did I care about each child?
And they answer,
I tried.
I hope so.
I think I did.

Each year there is one school ending
more final than the others—
seniors graduate
with ceremony—

cap-and-gown processions
and hurrahs.

But one school ending caps all others—
the last hurrah,
the really final ending—

a teacher retires!

Students and colleagues pause
to celebrate memories
they will use
and pass on.

But this ending
has no cap-and-gown honors
no solemn procession.

Just the teacher
alone.
Standing there.

Standing on years of teaching,
receiving praise and thanks,
sharing the past,
saying goodbye.
And when empty silence comes,
the teacher wonders
Did I do all I hoped to do?
Did I do it well?

Did I love every child
—no matter what?
And the answer comes back:
    I tried.
I hope so.
    I think I did.

Now the teacher faces the final test:
Was it worth
all the time and trouble?
and the answer comes quickly,
    Oh, yes!
    I knew it would be!

                May 31, 2014

To My Brother, William Findley
Professor Emeritus, Brown University, May 28, 1983

    Long days and long hours of deep cogitation
        to dredge up solutions...
    long years and long hours dedicated to teaching—
        devotion to students...
    long hours and minutes of fine-tuning care
        of clock-set equipment.

    In office, in classroom, in well-ordered lab
        with quiet, thoughtful voice...
    in car or in cab, on plane or on train
        to travel for conference...
    by phone or by lecture or scholarly paper
        to speak of ideas.

    Now comes a brief moment of high recognition
        for all of these labors.
    Bill Findley joins others: Professor Emeritus,
        Brown University.

    Unable to be there I write of this honor
        to my brother William.
    I send my great pride and my joy and my love
        on this fine occasion!

Journeys beyond Walls

I'm spangled
with small sunny rainbows
doing daily exercises
on my bed
struggling as always
to make myself do
what's needed
not just
what's fun.

In a couple of minutes
I'll change
from pajamas
to shirt and slacks
and although
I'll be in a
different room
and I'll look
a bit different,
I'll still be myself.

* *

Yesterday I was in a hotel room
in a far-off city.
Like my rooms at home
it, too, had four walls
but instead of prisms

throwing rainbows
across the bed
there was only
the hard glare of sunlight.
But that didn't matter.
I was still myself
still making myself do
what was needed.

Soon I would go
to my brother's
memorial service.

* *

A week ago he was alive,
thriving
on chips and ice cream
and conversations
with any and all visitors
especially family,
regardless
of his stroke-slurred speech.

He was his secure self
inside his usual suit and tie
in his now-familiar
nursing home room
inside its protective walls,
still making his body do
what was needed.
* *

In death
he has continued to do
what is needed.
He has left behind
human walls
his beloved family
his suit and tie
and his worn body,
so desperately in need
of replacement—
something he no longer
needs.

What remains forever
is his generous soul,
his central reality.
He is still himself—Paul Findley.
But now,
free of all walls,
knowing love
beyond imagining,
he is gifted with
the full realization
of what is universal,
what is eternal,
and what is
ultimately
needed.

August 16, 2019

Jim

The phone rang late.

"Hello," I said,
wondering.

It was my niece.
"Dad died this afternoon."

My sister's husband
with eighty-nine years of
healthy, busy life
had been leveled
by the bite
of a tick.

Living alone many years
without his
beloved wife,
my vibrant
caring
sister.

Living alone at Long Island's
ocean tip
in a home he had
built,
three nails
where two would do.

A rare, good man
serving others:
lanky,
gentle,
hesitant,
thoughtful,
keen perfectionist
in some things.

Easily reminded of
apt stories.
Starting to laugh
in the telling.

Kind stories,
funny.

A church minister
full of joy
on Sundays
when the sermon
was over.

Genuine,
unconditional
in his warm enjoyment
of family
of all people.

A transparent
servant
of God.

We loved him.

> July 16, 2010

Rose Branches

Blood red,
the roses last year
swayed on their stems,
breathing out
tender perfume.

But winter's
cold shafts of ice
shattered the vines of life
left hollow death.

Spring came
and pruning shears
cut at the thorny arms,
tearing loose
death-stiffened brambles.

Blood red
the rose branches glow,
writhing in flames,
while gray moving shadows
enfold them.

June, 1959

The Almond Tree

It's April,
and outside my window,
decked in delicate pink blossoms,
the almond tree stands
motionless.

Suddenly, mysteriously,
one fragile blossom flutters.
Then another.
Then another.

I am entranced.
Each brief dance
is a sweet surprise—
sudden,
random.

My Almond tree in bloom

Of course, the cause is
an invasion of scattered raindrops
—truants from the sky.

These small dances bring to mind
the servant bells
in manor-house basements,
each bell dangling
from a curly spring.

Unseen in a room above,
someone pulls a tasseled cord,
and with each pull a mystery—
one of the springs below
jiggles its bell.
Soon another rings;
then another,
and at each dancing call
a servant departs
to answer the summons.

Just so the mystery of death
comes to each of us,
suddenly,
randomly
—the summoner unseen,
the departure immediate,
the only sign the vanished soul.

Like the blossom,
the bell-spring,
and the servant,
we respond.

May, 2015

Time

Time has set a windlass
turning the spiral of my days,
turning seconds into minutes,
hours into days,
years into eternity.

And the windlass twists
the filaments of life,
spinning me from out the past,
rising slowly,
spinning lightly,
out of dim remoteness
into birth,
into youth,
into age,
into dim remoteness—
a thin thin line
pulling ever upward,
gently turning.

What wonder
to gaze downward, upward,
seeing how changing
yet also changeless
the spiraling threads—
always learning,
losing,

brightening,
fading

rising.

1974

My peach tree in bloom

Easter Spring

Three weeks ago
the earth was winter-cold
and barren brown.

And then last week
green spears shot up.
Daffodils
bloomed bright yellow
and tiny spring flowers
spread about in patches
of brilliant blue,
coloring the drab earth.

We hardly notice
change from night to day
or rain to sun,
but when spring comes,
with its green life, its colors,
thrusting at last
out of the dead brown
of winter—
this change
does get our attention.

Only the creator
can really say why
the seasons change.

Perhaps it is to show us that
Jesus' life out of death,
Easter,
is truth
—yet another joyous return
of warm life
emerging from
the secrets of cold death
—now openly,
poignantly,
unforgettably.

—so we will wonder
and doubt
and marvel
at the hidden mystery
of death
and eternity

—so we will
pay attention to
Jesus' shining words:
love God,
yourself,
your neighbor,
your enemy

—so we can know our
oneness with God
and the earth's people,
and know
that God is love,
and unconditional love
is God.

Always.

2021

Love without Walls

*Treat others
as you would have others
treat you.*
The Golden Rule
is an expression of love
—caring and concern—
honored among
all the world's religions
—although a few extend this love
only to their own members.

Some faiths also limit their love
by worshiping a god
who loves only the good
and obedient,
not the treacherous
or sinful.

This is conditional love,
a love that builds walls
to keep some in
and keep others out.

Of course, any religion may have
individual members
who, in privacy,
actually prefer conditional love
because its boundaries

embrace only the godly,
the chosen.

After all,
when we think we are chosen
above others,
we feel good.

Unfortunately,
conditional love
can also make it tempting
to scorn or persecute
—even torture or kill—
people who don't
conform.

But there is
another kind of love
—UN-conditional love.
Jesus taught it:
God is love.
Love God.
Love your neighbor
as yourself.
Love your enemies.

No walls.

When love has no walls,
each of us matters
—and all of us

fallible humans
need boundless love.
Unconditional love.

Such love is not easy.
But if you and I
can love someone
who chooses to harm others
—someone we understand,
someone precious to us,
(NOT loving or supporting
the harm, of course,
and wanting to make repairs)

—if you and I can love thus,
then, perhaps,
some day
everyone in our whole world
will learn to reach
across the prickly barriers
of religion,
to love each other
unconditionally.

To love without walls.

If that should ever happen,
we will have peace.
Real, lasting
peace.

January, 2022

Three Gifts

There are times in our lives
when we look deeply, deeply within,
and examine our souls:
when our children are born
and when
our loved ones die.

At the time of
the joyful miracle
of birth
we scrub out our souls
and promise the child
the gift of our unconditional love
—and sunshine days
and starry nights
forever—
a promise we cannot keep.

But when it's time for
the miracle of death
for one
whose gift of unconditional love
has enriched our lives,
we find their gift
has so cleansed and stretched
our souls
that in this time of loss

our reach goes far beyond
promises,
even beyond the singing stars,
to touch
the warmth
of God's great gift
of love.

November 7, 2016

War and Peace

The air was sweet and warm.
From our bench by the lake
we watched a small family
wander along the shore
hearing their faint voices
exclaiming over each
newly-discovered shell

Behind their dark figures
the radiant
sun-bathed lake and sky
glowed in merging shades
of pink and magenta
as the sun slipped silently
toward the edge of the world

This was peace—

The riverboat cabin was stifling hot.
The baby
was screaming
and our three-year-old
had just decided
he could pour his own glass of milk

But his project had crashed.
Both bottle and glass

were rolling about in a pool of milk
that was drowning the whole table
and splashing down
onto the floor.

My husband lashed out at me
"Can't you make her be quiet?"

"Go sit in time out!"
I yelled at the three-year-old.
"Why are you
always making a mess?"
This was WAR!

Luckily,
a card I'd stuck on the refrigerator
caught my eye:
"Problem Solving," it announced.
"Try to understand.
Use words that help."

I retrenched.
"Wait!" I said to our weeping boy.
"It's OK."
I hugged him tight.
"I'm sorry.
I know you didn't mean
to make a mess."

My husband retrenched.
"I'm sorry, too" he said,

reaching for our unhappy little girl.
"Let me take her out on deck."

We smiled.
This was peace—

Peace comes to us in two kinds:

Sometimes,
peace is a mirrored lake.

Usually, though,
peace is a rolling river
flowing unstoppable
through random dangers
but staying carefully and lovingly
within its banks.

Both are beautiful.

2018

Wedding Gift

On this lighthearted
ringing day,
you come together,
warmly hand in hand,
to share your love
in vows
to care
for each other
in married life
with tender love,
bringing special joy
to family and friends
and bustling world
with solemn pledge
and sunshine feast
and joyful dance
to celebrate your
special,
wondrous,
wedding gift from God
—your love.

February, 2019

My maple leaves at dusk

Return

In the dusk beyond the window
golden leaves
flicker on dark brown branches,
each leaf a miniature flame
from the sun.

The autumn sun slants low,
casting long shadows,
warning of frozen days
to come.

Now it grows darker.
Still the glowing leaves
smile through the gloom,
smiling of summer sun,
smiling the promise
hidden behind each stem,—
the promise
of far-off, budding spring.

In my own autumn
of slanting shadow,
I embrace each bright moment,
loving all the golden faces,
hugging tight the promise—
winter's hidden promise
of a far-off return

to golden faces,
a return
to this shining life.

      October 10, 2011

Small Bully

Nailed to the tree outside my window
is a miniature wooden table
with a tiny seat attached behind it.
As a table it's unique,
for it has a long, sharp spike
sticking straight up out of its middle,
just the right size
for an ear of corn.

Every day I find a member
of our squirrel family
seated at the table,
a small mock-human.
With great delicacy,
he bites off a kernel,
clutches it in his little squirrel fingers,
and nibbles away with delicate zest
—a fastidious diner!

But he's not always so polite.

The time I forgot his ear of corn
he glared at me through the window,
jerking his frothy golden-brown tail
back and forth,
stamping his fist-paws on the table
—a "chairman of the board"

cherking loudly at me in ferocious anger,
bullying me with death threats
for my neglect.

Outdone by his superior will,
I meekly surrendered
to the furry little spitfire
and gave him his ear of corn
—quite willing to be bullied
since he was only one-tenth my size
and his teeth were on
the other side of the window.

Besides, I owed it to him.
I'm the one who taught him
to prostitute his wild charms
for treats.

January, 2020

The Pea-Pickin' Song
Fort Collins, Colorado, July 7, 1983
Barbara and Miriam,
Kristen, and Ruthann

Sittin' in the pea patch,
pickin' all the peas.
Sittin' in the pea patch,
Miriam and me.
One pod,
two pods,
three pods,
four.
Sittin'
in the pea patch,
gettin' stiff and sore.

Peeps Bunnies

I bought two packages of Peeps bunnies today,
the kind that are like flat yellow snowmen
with ears straight up.
I ate four already.

I don't eat the thick ones squatted over.
They don't have the ears and
being thick makes them too squishy.
I tried pink and purple bunnies with ears,
but they didn't taste nearly as good as yellow
and the colors seemed wrong.
I even tried the white Christmas Peeps snowmen.
You can have them.
No, it's just the yellow bunnies with ears.

Why I like them of course is the great taste
and the crunchy sugar coat;
but what I like best
is the ears—
the fun of eating one ear and then the other.

My kids always liked
eating the hands and feet and head
off the pancake men I used to make,
so maybe there is something about having
a bit sticking out
that's the right size for biting off
that makes it fun.

Anyhow I'm 86 and I like eating Peeps bunnies ears first.
I guess joy is in the small things.
I guess joy is where you find it.

                                      March 29, 2015

Addiction

Just now insomnia
has invaded my night
as usual,
so I'm trying my favorite gimmick
for going back to sleep.

I'm doing Sudoku puzzles.

Here's my plan:
fifteen minutes of filling squares
with numbers 1 to 9
will deaden my brain
and I'll fall asleep from boredom.

Unfortunately,
I usually have too much fun.
Party fun.
Little tricks for finding
the number I need
and then I sock 5 or 6 others
into place.

Cheers! Sky rockets!
It's an addiction.

Here's what happens too often:

Puzzle and pencil fall.
I'm at last nodding off.
But then
—*hard to believe I'd do this!*—
instead of letting go
I'll actually
pull myself back
from that sleep
I need so desperately
Just so I can
fill in those squares!
Just so I can
"feel good!"

Here I am, eighty six
—old enough to be wise—
sleep-deprived
and knowing it,
and what am I telling myself?
Wait…
Don't stop…
I want the sky rocket!

It's an addiction.

The only difference
between me
and the dangerous addicts
is that I'm addicted to Sudoku
instead of whisky
or heroin.

So I scold myself.
I try logic.
Think of all the things
you want to do
in the time you have left.
Remember, you'll be too tired tomorrow
to do anything.
And remember, it isn't just about you.
You're linked tight
to those you love.
Things that damage you
could damage them somehow.

Then I get tough.
I give myself orders.
Let go of the fun
Let go of the sky rockets
Use the brain God gave you!

And sometimes I do actually
use it....

May, 2013

You Are What You Eat, or Miracle Cure!

Growing old
is a tilting fun-house—
full of surprises.

When chronic diarrhea
reduced me when eighty
from a hundred and twenty
to ninety pounds
    (My family hates
    that word diarrhea.
    "Not out loud!
    they cry in disgust.)
I got a new diet of
rice and beans,
rice and beans,
and gained back up
to a hundred and twenty.

A miracle cure!

But as I grew used to
my wonderful diet,
    (It was always the same
    under different names:
    Rice Milanese
    and Jambalaya
    are rice and beans,
    rice and beans.)
I began to notice
a mutiny rising again,
deep down.

And after a while,
I was back
once more
to ninety pounds,
ninety pounds.
"This is it perhaps!"
I thought,
getting thinner
and thinner
    while trying
    new versions
    of rice and beans,
    rice and beans.

But rescue arrived.

The ubiquitous cell phone
with all of its apps
revealed a miracle
straight out of Stanford
—a brand new diet
that zaps diarrhea!

"No more
rice and beans,
rice and beans,
ever again!
Steak, fish, chicken, cheese!
Steak, fish, chicken, cheese!
Hooray!" I cried

    And soon
    I started to work back up
    to a hundred and twenty

    A miracle cure!

    * *

So now
what happens
tomorrow?
    Oh, yes.
        Tomorrow…

                April 28, 2018

Cookie Jar

When my mother died
she was almost 107
and living in Colorado,
but her burial plot
was far away in Illinois,
waiting for many years
with its stone and my father.

She had asked for cremation,
perhaps to be practical
—but perhaps also
for its spare neatness.

Very wise, I thought.
Simple.

My niece, who is a potter,
provided the urn—
a repurposed cookie jar
—lovely blue-gray pottery
that would have pleased
the artist in Mom.

But the government routinely
ships bodies of soldiers home
from around the globe.
Even a soldier missing

years ago in the Korean War
was sent home last month,
his bones only.

Their families
speak of needing closure,
feeling that
only the tangible body
will answer
—which makes me wonder
about sailors buried at sea.

It shouldn't really matter
where the graves of war lie,
and yet I am always
moved to tears
to see the thousands
of white crosses
stretched in tight rows
to the horizon
in Gettysburg
in France
in Arlington.
No other symbol
so vividly mourns the lost sons,
      their terror,
      their agony,
their courage,
the waste.

No life should end without
celebrating
this great adventure.
Unthinking,
we use frozen custom
or religious ceremony.
But whether our symbol
is the body
or a portrait
or just words,
it is the living
face and form and spirit
that we have loved
and warmly hugged
that we celebrate
and mourn.

I'm glad we had Mom's ashes
in the beautiful urn
for her memorial,
marked with her name and dates
in front of us next to her portrait,
next to her kind,
beloved face.
I'm glad of ashes, too,
for it's not her body
but her timeless
loving soul
that remains,
that matters.

March 13, 2019

My Mom
Florence Nichols Findley

To Hold My Hand: My Mom
Florence Mary Nichols Findley

She told me once
that when I was a baby,
my crib was next to her bed
and she would hold my hand
in the dark.

When I had poison ivy
all over me,
she stayed by me all night,
putting lotion on my burning skin.

When I needed
to make a leaf collection for school,
we walked all over town together.
It was fun.
But anything I got credit for—
    like my 4H projects—
had to be my work only.

If I was in a special program
she was there,
even though we had no car
and she had to walk,
    whatever the distance.
She did this after walking hard floors
all day at work,
bossing the high school cafeteria kids

  —kids she worried about
  like her own.

She always welcomed my friends
to come and stay and eat and sleep.
And if I worried
about going to a party,
she would say "Just be yourself."
And she let me have a cat,
even though she didn't really like cats.

She was 42 when I was born
  —a big surprise
  since the rest of us
  ranged from 7 to 15 years old—
but she told me
she was always glad she had me,

and I knew she meant it.
I don't think she had a favorite
among the five of us.
It seemed to be
each of us in turn.
I guess we were all
her "favorite child."

I never once heard her complain
even though we sometimes had
nothing in the house to eat

but bread and milk.
    She would just fix toast
    and bread pudding.
And there was a time
she had only one pair of shoes
with soles worn so thin
they were patched over and over.

But she could be very firm.
Once when she thought
I was lying to her
    —I wasn't
    Well, not exactly—
she wouldn't let me go see
Shirley Temple in The Little Colonel,
    my first chance ever
    to see a movie
—a crushing punishment.

She never yelled or spanked.
She just handed out
penalties that fit,
and saw to it that we were
faithful church members.

Truth mattered to my mom
and responsibility
and loving kindness.
She helped me stand on my own
but I knew

if I ever needed it,
she would be there
to hold my hand.

April 24, 2018

No Complaints
Florence and Joe Findley

When the banks collapsed
in the 1930s and I was four,
my father lost all he had saved
and soon thereafter
contracted Parkinson's disease.
He was from then on
an invalid, home all the time.

He didn't complain about it,
but I'm told he yelled at me at first!
And Mom,
now mom, nurse, and breadwinner,
didn't complain either.

At first Mom
raised and sold vegetables,
working a large garden
eight blocks away,
starting at 5 a.m.,
often on 100-degree days.

Even so, she read to us every night
for fun,
after a long day's work,
often slurring off to sleep,
and we would urge her,
"Read, Mama! Read!"

A former star turn
doing readings in school assemblies,
she was really good!
We laughed ourselves helpless
over Huck Finn.

Soon she got a cooler job
managing an ice cream shop.
I remember well
a pumpkin pie
made totally of ice cream!

And then she managed the
Jacksonville, Illinois,
high school cafeteria—
"Mom" to all student help.
After school as a 6th and 7th grader,
I hobnobbed with her helpers,
learned how to tap dance
from the janitor, and
chatted with leftover teachers.

Then Mom's parents died
and we moved to their house
in Princeton (IL)
and Mom became a landlady
renting out the upstairs
until Pop died
after 20 years of Parkinson's.

We were poor.
No frills.
Our motto was, "We can't afford it."
This was not a complaint,
just the scraped-off truth.

All my clothes except shoes
were hand-me-downs
until I was a college senior.

Parkinson's
wasn't Pop's first "failure."
Before I was born
he had failed at farming.
When times were so hard
in the Great Depression,
my 10-year-old brother
became his sole hired man—
so lightweight
he had to stand
on the tractor pedal
with both feet
to shift gears.

Pop didn't complain, but
this failure had a double sting—
the losses hurt Mom's mother.
It was her farm.
So now, Pop,
a Methodist

with a year at
Purdue University,
became, instead of a farmer,
a substitute Presbyterian minister
and a YMCA director
and finally a door-to-door
life insurance salesman
who loaned his clients
their weekly payment
when they lacked the five cents.

Parkinson's disease and
the bank failure
left Pop with nothing except
a $50-a-month insurance dividend.
But we heard no complaints.

So now Mom carried on.
Growing up around
her "Doctor-Grandma,"
she had wanted to go to college.
But her father, son of that
"first woman doctor in Illinois,"
actually thought
his daughter
didn't need to go to college!

But like her grandma,
Mom "did it anyway"
—a year studying art

at Wheaton College,
earning her own way babysitting,
with pride, no complaints.

After two years of teaching
grade school
and china painting,
she met Pop at a church camp.
We three daughters and two sons
ALL went to college!
We "worked our way through"
and helped each other
pay expenses,
becoming four teachers
and one congressman.

Mom had wanted to be
an archeologist.
Instead, she became a mother.
Instead she took care of Pop
    and backed the rest of us.
Pop had wanted to keep on working.
Instead he patiently accepted
his helplessness.

They both helped us stand alone.
They both honored and cared about
their family and each other
and truth and hard work
and the unconditional love
that is God.

I never heard either of them
complain.

April 23, 2020

A Pair of Stockings

When I returned
to the hospital
from my walk,
my father's bed was empty—
tight-sheeted
and cold.

Before leaving his room
I had taken the folded money
from his
always wavering
fingers.

He had given me
his sharp, quick glance,
sealing my promise
to buy my mother
a pair of stockings
for her birthday,
always his gift,
always with me as agent,
always of utmost importance
to him,
locked as he was
into the relentless restraints
of Parkinson's disease—
always dependent
on others.

And suddenly
I had wanted to get out,
wanted just to
walk around the block,
wanted the everyday feel
of city streets and sidewalks.

We had been called to come
in the middle of the night
because my father
was not expected to live.

All during the long hours
driving north
with my brother
through the dark
of early morning,
I had stared
at the stark silhouettes
of trees
lining the horizon
against the endless sky,
thinking about death.

Now in the empty room
I fingered the wadded bills
my father had given me
to buy my mother
—to buy his wife—
a pair of stockings

for her birthday
next week.

But I had not
been there
to say goodbye.

May, 2017

How Clever

I wrote down the words.
"How clever of me,"
I thought.

How ugly it is
to be proud
of being
clever.

1965

Words

Yesterday I bought a thesaurus
to help me find
the very best words.

Not just any old thesaurus—
the huge new
Roget's International Thesaurus,
325,000 words
I can use
if I want to.

Even in paperback
that many words are pretty hefty—
about the weight of a fat cat.

I must say that having this
plethora of words in my hands,
weighty though it is,
is lots more fun
than messing around with
my fickle computer.

I can just flip its pages and
browse/scan/skim/
the mesmerizing
words

—hundreds of options
right there before my eyes.

It's simple to find
the ultimate best word,
since this thesaurus
has rounded up the entire universe
of English words
into families,
starting with
"body."

And the first word under body
—the elemental word
among all words—
is
—what else?
"Birth!"
the all-time
First Word.

After all,
at the birth
of our universe,
words were all we had.
(John 1:1)
In the beginning
was the Word
and the Word was with God
and the Word was God.

So,
when I hold this thesaurus
    in my hands,
I am holding
not just
thousands of words.
In a way
I am holding
the entire universe.

In a way
I am holding
something of
God.

Something
way beyond
words.

                    For Zachary
                    June, 2015

The Sculptured Poem

The trouble
with a poem
is
it comes with
its own demands.

The moment you set down
a few lines,
the poem takes over,
    demanding this detail,
    that pattern,
    this and that idea,
until suddenly
what you have is
much too much muchness
sprawling all over,
so that the whole thing
becomes a matter of
asking yourself,
    "What on earth
      am I trying to say?"

After all, you do
have to be saying
something
—or why the poem?

As it is
you're probably
saying
far too many things;

or perhaps
nothing at all.

But here's the beauty:

While probing the muddle
for meaning,
you may
come up with a nugget
that is something
new
or important—
    even beautiful—

or maybe not.

But at least now,
you know better
what you have
and where to
    build
    and sort

   and trim
until at last
the poem sits there,
solid
in its own person.

Like a sculptor
chipping away
at a block of marble,
you have found your vision
at its heart.

And if you're lucky,
it's a poem
worth
keeping.

                                May, 2017

The Path Ahead

The path I follow comes to an end
up ahead beyond the woods.

And I...am I afraid?

No, not afraid
of what lies behind the woods.
Truth—light—lies there.

No, not afraid.
But I know
the path through the woods
may crumble away,
and before I can reach the light,
there may be falls
    and stumbles
—a drain on those I love.

But I know, too,
that what matters
is that the light is there for me
and there for them.

What matters is that the light
is with me, unseen
as I follow my path.

What matters is that my path
takes me where I will at last
see the light.

My mind reaches out.
I follow my path through the woods
    toward the light,
      the truth,
the infinite, unconditional love
that is God.

                            December 12, 2012

Passageways

Seated on Sunday
beside stained-glass windows,
he bows his head
with the others
in silence.

Kneeling alone
in accustomed humility,
she whispers "Hail, Mary"
fingering beads.

Folded comfortably
into lotus position,
he chants
humming monotony.

Lying in trance,
the clairvoyant
transmits knowledge
from the
universal consciousness
to those beside him.

Fashioned
from the singing clouds,
the luminous earth
gives us lives of both
joy
and pain,
challenging us to learn
unselfish love,

while giving
within each life,
time for seeking
again and again
the hidden soul's
passageway
to God—
    perhaps
    at last
    to know.

July, 2015

Lion out of Bounds

It is midnight,
January cold.

Hard-driven snow
beats against
our window panes.

Suddenly—
startling in the wintry dark—
the whole house
is shaken
by a menacing roar
of summer thunder,
roaring like a hungry
African lion on the hunt,
prowling about
our snowy yard
—nature out of place,
out of bounds.

Inside our safe walls
small primeval fears
whisper.

* *

Tomorrow
the thunderstorm
will be over,
the disturbing thunder
but a memory.

But other prowling lions,
other fears,
will circle our lives,
growling
at the backs of our minds—
9-11 terrorists
corruption,
global warming,
COVID-19—
roaring out of bounds,
seeking prey.

Where is God?
These dangers we fear
are our own creation,
not God's—
dangers born of self-love
broken out of bounds.

God is within us,
stronger than any fear.
Instead of a roaming
rescue squad,

God has given us
universal laws,
eternal love,
our souls,
our freedom,
our minds.

When we choose in truth
and freedom
to search within,
we find his boundless love—
love that greets us
with outstretched peace,
peace that calms
our roaring fears.

Why, then, do we wait
until the dark lion
is roaring out of bounds?

January 30, 2008

Red Balloon

I was four and very excited,
all by myself in the back yard
batting a big, bouncy red balloon
up into the bright sunshine
—my very first balloon!

Then in a single instant
there was a deafening explosion
directly in front of my face,
and my beautiful balloon
vanished.

I shook with terror.

From then on,
anything that might explode
with a bang
made me tremble

—until I took voice lessons
at age thirty.

This is not the leap it seems,
for this teacher
taught me to relax my jaw,
and I found I could now
endure,

even enjoy
any and all explosive
bangs.

I have often thought
how glad I am
that my teacher knew
how to relax jaw muscles
and was patient enough
to teach me.

He said my brother William and I
had the tightest-clenched jaws
he'd ever known.

Of course,
when you think about it,
I owe just as much gratitude
to the person
who taught my teacher
      and even more
to that original genius
      who figured out
how to relax the jaw
in the first place
—all of which leads ultimately
to the creative force
that guided our evolution
with such love
that we have minds and bodies

so intricate
we're able to learn to control
the obscure muscles
of the jaw!

In fact, once you think about it,
all that we have on earth
springs from countless minds
and recedes to our creator—
like the trick image of a girl
    holding a picture of herself
        holding a picture of herself,
           until girl and picture
              gradually shrink into
                mysterious infinity.

What a nameless marvel
is this world,
this bouncy life
we enjoy so carelessly!

                        May 18, 2019

Fireworks: Gabriel Kusch and his Great Uncle Dave Stuart watch

Fireworks

It's the 4th of July.
Independence Day!
Very hot,
very humid,
even now at night.

I hurry along the sidewalk,
one of thousands
streaming toward the park.

We are the fireworks crowd.
We are "the people,"
the government
"of, by, and for the people."

We are the
moving, singing, talking,
t-shirted people,
created equal in rights
"to life, liberty, and
the pursuit of happiness."

I love the fireworks,
the shimmering fantasies
filling the sky.

I love the great white "Boom!"
of the flash-bombs
filling me so tight with sound

I am a drum,
vibrating with freedom.

But I love most
being merged
with the crowd,

feeling a oneness
with the people I pass by
and move with
and sit among—
toddlers and
wandering teens and
families on the grass,
a warm melt
of black, white, brown,
old and young
rich and poor,
pulled and mixed
together
for the 4th of July—

all of us here
to celebrate freedom
and equal rights,

something
so beyond words
that only fireworks
will answer.

July, 2007

9-11: New York

The sunlit towers soar,
trim, pristine, powerful,
sheltering
mothers, husbands,
sisters, sons,
here from home
to transact
the world's business.

Now,
in a searing,
hate-fueled inferno,
these thousands,
these beloved innocents,
vanish
into thundering clouds

of ash
and released spirit.

Frozen with terror,
we watch
as the giant towers
dissolve before us.

Only anguish remains:
for this brutal holocaust,
endless horror;
for these fragile ashes,
tears that burn;
for these vanished souls,
our emptiness.

September 11, 2001

9-11: Pennsylvania

Four silver planes,
giant bullets
bearing fiery destruction,
streak though sunny skies,
captured by fierce hatred
secretly targeting
freedom,
targeting the flawed, free people
leading America.

These four planes carry
businessmen,
technicians,
mothers with children,
flying
to attend meetings,
see a new baby,
or just come back home.

Ordinary, everyday people—
not soldiers,
not trained rescuers
    pledged to sacrifice—
just ordinary people
pledged to love their family,
pledged to love their freedom,
pledged to love.

Now on one plane of the four—
one plane
flying above the hills
  of Pennsylvania—
now these ordinary people
know their mission,
know horror,
know they are a living weapon
aimed at the heart of America
aimed at the government
  of, by, and for the people,
aimed at the people chosen by vote,
gathered in the capitol
to govern us.

These ordinary people
now lean on their love,
searching among themselves
for a plan,
calling their loved ones to say,
Goodbye.
I love you.
Remember me.
Not much time.
We're going to vote.
Goodbye.
I love you.

These ordinary people
pledged to love,

pledged to freedom,
these ordinary Americans
now vote,
vote to unite,
vote to rush to meet fiery death,
vote to rescue
our government.

A shout goes up,
"Let's roll!"

And the phones go silent.

There is no greater love
than this:
to give our lives
for freedom;
to give our lives
for love.

September 11, 2011

Killing George Floyd
(May 28, 2020)

The sidewalk bystanders
watch, unbelieving,
as a strong, tall Black man,
lying shackled on the sunny street,
is gradually killed by white police
before their eyes.

One cop has his knee
on the Black man's neck,
and keeps it there,
and keeps it there.
more than nine long minutes,
ignoring the Black man
as he begs
over and over,
I can't breathe!
I can't breathe! Please stop!

The bystanders
call out desperately,
trying to save him.

But the white policeman,
hand in pocket, arrogant,
ignores them.
He has power!

So he presses his knee
into the Black man's neck
and keeps pressing
and keeps pressing—
long after the Black man's
pleadings have died away,
long after breath is gone,
long after death has come.

They had arrested
George Floyd
only on suspicion
of deliberately using
a counterfeit $20 bill
to buy cigarettes.
But George Floyd
resisted arrest.
So they killed him.
Then they reported his death
as an accident.
As usual.

But a brave young Black girl
had made a video
of every minute.
And soon the world knew.

The Black and Brown world
wept
and gathered with others

to protest
and protest
day after day
until at last
Justice paid attention
and there was a court trial!

The world watched the trial
because no white cop
had ever been
successfully tried anywhere
for murdering a Black man.
Not ever.

The brave sidewalk watchers
and the brave
white police chief
and a brave
white expert doctor
testified,
and the truth was known.
The brave jury said "Guilty!"
and the murderer
went to prison
for a long time—
much longer than
nine minutes.

The Black and Brown world
shouted for joy

and was happy
for a day or two.
But this was just
one Black man.
Just one time.
Just a beginning.

Even so,
there was a flicker of hope
—hope for real change
this time.

Real change will be
slow and hard
because all who run
toward justice
are seeking fairness
and equal rights,
and the hurdles on this track
are high—
hurdles of whites fearing
loss of power
and Blacks fearing
more denial
of justice and jobs,
and both fearing death.

But if we clear these hurdles,
the white-hot hate
forged from these fears
will cool.

Real change will be
slow and hard
because only love
can cast out fear—
love that cares equally
about the inner worth
of each person.
Such love seems
impossible
in this world.

And yet, perhaps…

if brave leaders will
step outside their safe-boxes
to show equal love—
doing what's not easy—
and
if brave ordinary people
will show equal love openly—
doing what's not easy—
then perhaps,
at last,
this dark injustice
of centuries,
this great, festering wound
will heal.

June 11, 2021

Anger is a Frightened Horse

Anger is a frightened horse
with tossing head,
flashing eyes
and slashing hooves—
a wild, overpowering beauty
too easily unleashed
in sudden madness.

Gentleness can soothe its fright.
But if no one cares
if no firm hand catches it

anger must then rush into tangled darkness
and pant
and scream,
trumpeting terror,
seeing menacing shadows
on all sides,
trampling into the dust
the soft creatures in its path—

to stand trembling at last
with heaving sides
quiet,
but still pursued
by fear.

1955

Traffic Ticket

He forgot his car lights
when he left Pub II.
The cop grabbed him hard,
pushed him backward
over the engine—
nose to nose smelling his breath.
    No alcohol.
No arrest.
No apology.
All for nothing but fear.

The police dog barked.
The cop searched his car,
tore apart his sound speakers,
threw his stuff all over.
    No drugs.
No arrest.
No cleanup.
No apology.
All for nothing but fear.

He asked for a complaint form.
"What you want that for?"
the desk cop asked.
"Better watch what you write."
He wrote it anyhow.
    No response.
All for nothing but fear.

But now when he's driving,
it's not long before he notices
flashing red and white lights
in the rearview mirror.

Turn signals too late again?
Driving while Black of course.

Another traffic ticket.
All for nothing
    except fear.

                           August, 2018

Travel

I don't need to travel!

I can stay right here
and go on an African safari just by
watching a fierce kitten
pounce to kill a twitchy string,
or by tracking a hawk
as it soars across the blue,
or by stalking the gray crawdads
        hiding in our muddy creek.

There's no need to go
to the mountains to ski
when every winter brings
snowy rooftop peaks,
sleds racing down nearby slopes,
children plodding back up,
puffing steam.

Who needs foreign adventures
when we have five o'clock traffic
 on the belt line
and when tornado sirens
scream at us as we
crouch in the basement
under the ping-pong table
while wild winds and booming thunder
shake the house above us?

And nothing in the world is lovelier than
green lawns, white daisies, golden trees,
glistening wet streets
     streaked red from taillights,
or a sleeping baby.

I don't need to travel.

For Ruthann
February, 2012

George Stuart 1943, new Radioman 2nd Class

D-Day at Omaha Beach
George Warren Stuart, June 6, 1944

On D-Day at age twenty
he was one of a million
men and boys.

The ships swarmed
as far as he could see
under cold gray clouds
—nine hundred warships
heaving on choppy waters,
ships packed so solid
he thought to himself,
"I could walk on them all the way
from England to France, ship to ship"

He was one of a million
sons and husbands
thousands of miles from home, school, jobs,
with no sleep the night before
    from excitement,
        from facing tomorrow's unknown,
    from fear of death.

He was an American sailor
in the largest armada of all time,
here for a rare, just war,
invading Europe
to stop the crazed creator

    of the Nazi war,
    to stop him from ruling the world,
        from ending freedom and democracy,
    to stop his destruction of all Jewish people
        in mad mass extermination
        of gas and screams
        and mountains of naked bony corpses.

He was a radioman on D-Day
along with a thousand men and boys
jammed inside his mammoth LST
—a Landing Ship Transport
renamed by sailors "Long Slow Target" —
now a real target of murderous fire
from big guns on the cliffs above.
Now his LST, churning doggedly toward land,
hit Nazi sea-barriers and stopped too soon,
so the giant landing doors opened
on chin-deep water instead of the beach,
and soldiers with heavy backpacks drowned,
while survivors struggled through the surf,
thrust on by courage and desperation
through a barrage of deadly explosions,
toward the carnage of
Omaha Beach.

Amid the deafening roar of battle
he sent and received, sent and received

his radio messages,
and soon the LST turned awkwardly,
dodging death,
to go back
to get another
and another
and another load
of sons and husbands.

Again and again exploding shells
hit his LST—the long slow target—
until at last he was blown into the sea
where a wounded sailor died beside him;
but rescue came in time for him,
and in the hospital,
at last,
there was silence.

And he kept his life.

But from that day,
whenever he shut his eyes to sleep,
the deaths of D-Day
played over and over—
the ceaseless roar of gunfire
the screams of the wounded
and the dead
—stone-eyed and washed clean
in the red-stained waters
of Omaha Beach.

And he couldn't sleep.

He was one
of the million men and boys
of D-Day.

                June 6, 2016

A Winter's Tale

Snow fell softly, coldly,
into alleys, making drifts;
into the staring dead eyes
of a stubble-faced boy
splayed on the cold cement,
cold, bare fingers gripping
a wad of squashed paper money.

Snow fell on the dark red flow
seeping from under his cap.
and on the gray gun
with the finger still on its trigger—
the finger that had pulled hard
out of mixed excitement
and hate
and fear—
the finger that had pulled fast
because
another finger was tightening on
a blue gun's trigger.

And the snow brushed the blue gun
and sifted lightly over a dark blue suit
with silver buttons, a silver badge,
and a dark red stain.

Starry flakes were caught
in thick eyebrows
above surprised open eyes
and fell gently
onto a clean-shaven face
that would have glowed with life
but for the icy blue gun
that had frightened the gray gun.

Living figures stood
in the swirling snow
—angry faces under blue caps
gloved hands gripping blue guns
promising more death
from more guns.

1954

A Prayer for Our Government

Individual prayers were offered monthly
by McLean, Illinois, County Board members

    We thank you, oh God,
        for the gifts of the earth,
        for the gift of life,
        and for the ability to communicate
            with each other.

    Make us more aware of our need
        to listen well and to speak well
        so that we will better understand
            the problems we face
            and the solutions we choose.

    Teach us to search for truth
    and to be open to your guidance
    in all that we say and do.

    Remind us to be grateful
    for the vision of those who created this,
    our imperfect,
    yet liberating and inspiring government
    that respects the needs,
        the individuality,
        and the equal rights
        of all people.

Guide us so that,
even though we are sure to make mistakes,
we will still continue with the building
    of what has been begun
    in this great experiment,
    this government
        of, by, and for
        the people.

For it is only in being aware
of your great love
for all people
that we will be able to choose wisely
the path that we
will follow.

        Barbara Findley Stuart, Board Member
        For my last meeting, October, 1996

Puppeteer; 2017

In the elegant, presidential room,
his cabinet and advisers
surround the table
strangely silent and watchful,
controlled by the
smiling,
smiling
new president,
his blond hair precisely shaped.

Each in turn,
already a mere puppet
constrained by unaccustomed fear,
praises the new president,
expressing abject admiration,
slavish devotion.

The world watches, shocked,
alarmed,
unbelieving.
Is this a madman unleashed?
An old Mafia film?

The mesmerized millions
who voted for the puppeteer
worship him at frequent,
carefully-staged mass celebrations—

this man who so enchants them
that they eagerly await
each new day
to see what ruthless thing
he will do next to please them;
this man, whose insidious ridicule
and thrusts against his enemies
make them laugh and cheer;
this man who makes them feel
powerful and secure.

They do not seem to know that
as the puppeteer gains power,
the strings that pull them
will grip tighter
until enforced mass puppetry
becomes the future
they have chosen.

September 20, 2020

Right the Third Time
Charlottesville 2017

Today,
I bought a toy piano keyboard
for my little great-grandson.
It didn't work.
So I took it back.

I was wrong!
It works.
It's the volume control
that turns it on, dummy.
Not the "play" button!

Today, neither of my
remote keys
would unlock my car.
I thought something was wrong
with the lock system,
so I took the car to the dealer.

Wrong again!
In an unprecedented
suicide pact
both batteries were dying
together.

But also today,
my two stupidities were lost

in a swirling cloud
of nation-wide agonizing—
people struggling with words
to end an assault on our
bedrock equal rights
at Charlottesville.

It began as an orderly protest
against the removal of a statue
of Robert E Lee
because he was
a Civil War general
who has become a
symbol
of slave-owning
white supremacy.

But racial hatred
commandeered
the peaceful parade
as a stage
for a blatant public exhibition,
meticulously planned
by neo-Nazis and the Ku Klux Klan
to demean
and insult Jews and Blacks,
thereby fomenting outrage
among all of us
who care about equal rights.

Since their beginnings,
white supremacists
have waged vicious wars
to erase Jews from the earth
and return blacks
to abject submission—
all for one reason:
to reserve power and privilege
for themselves.

Now, hurling threats and insults,
parading white supremacy,
glorifying Civil War symbols
    of chains and slavery,
they unleashed insurrection
and innocent death.

Today, I, too, protest
through this poem,
protest for equal rights
and a peaceful solution
that will last.

This time, today, the third time,
I got things right!

August 17, 2017

'HIS LEGACY LIVES'

Merlin Kennedy, black trailblazer in B-N, dies at 92

BY DEREK BEIGH
derek.beigh@lee.net

BLOOMINGTON — A "true hero" to Bloomington-Normal's black community has died.

Merlin Kennedy, a past Bloomington-Normal NAACP president known for portraying Santa Claus in the Twin Cities' 1966 Christmas parade to protest its "One Santa" rule, passed away Friday at age 92.

"Mr. Kennedy was an icon and a great supporter of the NAACP," said NAACP President Linda Foster in a news release. "He kept NAACP relevant and engaged with the community, which propelled the NAACP to thrive in the Bloomington-Normal community. We have lost a true hero and he will be greatly missed, but his legacy lives on."

Kennedy helped pass a fair-housing ordinance, establish human relations commissions in Bloomington and Normal and integrate State Farm's hiring program.

In 1966, he was denied membership at a segregated American Legion post in the Twin Cities so he rode on a Memorial Day parade float with a sign, "Our war

In this Nov. 18, 2013, file photo, Kennedy displays a newspaper article that covered a 1967 talk he gave on the roots of racial tension in the Twin Cities.

dead died together. Bloomington segregated their honor today."

Later that year, he dressed as Santa on a float in the annual Christmas parade but police stopped the float and Kennedy and three others walked the route. The event made national news.

Kennedy was the first recipient of the Normal Human Relations Commission's Martin Luther King Jr. Award and in 1999 was given the NAACP's Roy Wilkins Award for his efforts to fight racism.

Twin City civil rights leader Henry Gay said Kennedy "was as dear to me as was Dr. Martin Luther King Jr." — "like a brother to me, and I could often finish his sentences for him."

"I moved to Bloomington in 1945, whereas he didn't come until 1959. When he got here, everything still was segregated," said Gay. "Merlin was a big part of that starting to change."

On the web

For a gallery of photos and previous Pantagraph stories, go to Pantagraph.com.

Gay said one of their major successes was a fair-housing ordinance, which meant "the slum landlords had to fix their places." He described an early residence where "you could sit in your living room and look at the stars."

"I would go at 2 o'clock in the morning to the outhouse at 19 below zero," said Gay. "We marched to show the community, 'We want jobs and a nice place to live in.' We want what they've got."

In those days, said Gay, "If you had a job and mentioned Martin Luther King Jr. or the NAACP, you'd get fired." But Kennedy was still an early leader, serving as president from 1962 to 1978.

"It was hard. Nothing changed overnight, but we kept going on," said Gay. "Merlin knew, you take your time, do things right and you can get something done."

Please see KENNEDY, Page A2

Kennedy

From A1

Gay still remembers vividly the "black Santa" moment.

"We were only in there on the float for 30 seconds, but we walked from Front Street to Miller Park, and you should've seen those kids' eyes. It was just like they were getting a toy," he said.

Barbara Stuart, a former McLean County Board member, former co-chair of the Minority Employment Council and longtime friend of Kennedy, said he will be remembered mostly for being the black Santa Claus "because it was such a vi... worked on together was a survey of black and white perceptions of fairness and treatment by Bloomington police.

He also was involved in a project that looked at the differences in how black couples and white couples were treated when trying to rent a house.

"He was quiet about what he did," she said, but "he was a very good man to have on a committee. He listened thoroughly ... and had good ideas."

Camille Taylor, a black longtime educator and community activist, said Kennedy's legacy extended into the next generation as well.

"I first heard about him through my work with the ... tray a black Santa at a time when the community did not view that in a positive way. It was groundbreaking and courageous. ... He showed all children and families Santa Claus is universal and doesn't have to be white."

Normal Mayor Chris Koos noted Kennedy was later featured as Santa Claus at Normal's Santa Station in 2013.

"I think it was a pretty important day for him, and a long time coming," said Koos. "The man did so incredible amount of heavy lifting early in his life and late in his life. He did that for his community."

Bloomington Mayor Tari Renner said Kennedy "was a pillar in our community ... to come."

"He always exemplified courage and also the kind of nonviolent movement that Dr. King pushed for that was so successful nationally ... even if it produced some shock value, and that was the point," said Renner.

"It was considered to be this in-your-face, terrible scandal. 'That's not what Santa Claus is about,'" he continued. "But he had the intended effect, forcing people to reexamine their own thought process, whether black or white."

Kibler-Brady-Ruestman Memorial Home, Bloomington, is assisting Kennedy's family with arrangements.

Contact Derek Beigh at (309) 820-3234 [...]

Merlin Kennedy: barrier breaker

123

Merlin Kennedy

His name is not the English wizard's
MER-lin.
His parents gave him
      an African lilt:
Mer-LIN is his name.
"Do you remember
when we got the 4-H fair
to quit selling racist t-shirts?"
I ask Merlin,
"The ones with the confederate flag?"
His almost blind eyes smile at me
from his nursing home bed.
"I sure do."
And he tells me
about working fifteen years
for a local founding family
—telling with love
how he sat with Lafayette Funk
as he died.
"I was a pall bearer," he says
with quiet pride.
Somehow,
as we talk of other times when
he flattened hurdles for his race
—somehow we fail to mention
the most tradition-flipping,
skyrocket day McLean County's

African Americans ever had
—the day he,
Merlin Kennedy,
decided that our Black children
needed to see a
Black Santa Claus
in the Christmas parade
      for a change
—that cold, historic Saturday
when angry white police
pulled him off his float—
a Black Santa in a red suit—
and made him walk
with the rest of the parade
on down the snowy street.
No, instead of that milestone,
Merlin speaks
in unbelieving tones
of a time when a group
honored him
by sending a representative
to take him out to dinner
once a month.
"They sent a woman," he tells me,
"a white woman,
and she sat with me
at a table in a restaurant
with white people all around
—every month"
The wonder

is rich in his voice
and in fact it's not long
before his mind
returns to that miracle year
—clearly it was
the very highest peak
of his long
revolutionary life.
"She was a white woman
and she sat at a table
with me
alone"
He says it again,
still amazed
almost beyond words
that such a thing
had happened
—that it had happened
to him,
that it had happened
to MerLIN Kennedy,
a Black man.

October 10, 2019

The Paul Findley Trail
or
The Lament of a Wagon-Sitter in Hardin County, Illinois, 1975 on a Congressman Findley Fundraiser

(Sung to "The Old Chisholm Trail)

Oh, come along folks and listen to my tale
And I'll tell you my troubles on the Paul Findley Trail.
    (Chorus) Come-a ti yi, yippee yippee yay, yippee yay!
    Come-a ti yi, yippee yippee yay!

Mr. Trail Boss Al is a mighty fine guy.
He can lay out a trail over bumps miles high!
    (Chorus)

The trail took us up on a very rough ridge
Where Lucille won fame playing wagon-trail bridge.
    (Chorus)

And there was Paul a-sittin' on Clancy
And he didn't fall off and he looked mighty fancy.
    (Chorus)

*   *   *

Now Paul's bunking down in Jacksonville city
And he's traded in Clancy for a little gray kitty!
    And its Hap-py Ninety-Second Birthday, Paul!
    On a Can-cun birthday jamboree!

John Lewis, Civil Rights Leader

Today,
America honored Congressman John Lewis.
We would not have so honored
      any Black man
when John was young.
But today,
partly because his faith and courage
helped gain the vote for Blacks—
      which helped John, himself,
      become a congressman—
today, things are better.

So it was, that on this 100-degree July day,
for the first time in history,
a congressman
      who was Black
was celebrated in a long funeral procession
through Washington D.C. to the capitol.

There, the two Black drivers of the hearse
stood proudly in the relentless sun,
until, in full-dress military uniform,
      Black service men and women
carried John's flag-draped coffin
with measured perfection
up each of forty steps
and into the rotunda to rest in honor
amid silent fellow congressmen and senators.

Now,
the Southern-white-male senate leader—
    usually an opponent of
    humane measures
    John has backed—
stood and spoke of John
with unaccustomed respect.
Then the Speaker of the House,
John's colleague—
    a white woman—
also spoke of John with respect—
but with added,
long-accustomed love and admiration.

The changes we saw today
in matters of honored positions—
    especially for Blacks—
happened in part because
John Lewis
had the vision and passion and courage,
    even as a youth,
    when he embraced
    what he called "good trouble,"
to join Martin Luther King's march
toward equal rights.

Facing the menacing dogs and
heavy clubs of Southern racists,
John led his people
across the Edmund Pettis Bridge

in peaceful non-resistance—
> doing that which was hard
>> and dangerous,
> meeting pain and violence
> without retaliation.

This matchless example of
> mass courage bonded to peace
won the amazed admiration and sympathy
of the nation—
and, thereby, won the vote.

Today, the Black vote still grows—
> now extended to women—
in spite of angry white efforts
to stop it.
But although great strides have been made
toward Black civil rights,
Many long miles remain.

*   *

It is not a fleeting, easy thing
> to embrace "good trouble."
It is not a soft, pointless thing
> to confront scorn and death
> with peaceful protest.
These are great, heroic things.

We salute you, John Lewis,
for these great things.

July 27, 2020

Ceremonies

When our heroes die
we celebrate them with
speeches,
poetry,
and music,
in places made festive
with flowers and flags.

We shout to the world,
"These are the things we value:
truth,
courage,
compassion."

We love ceremonies—
the comfort of tradition,
the feeling of accomplishment, and
the warmth of a happy gathering.

We love to celebrate also
the star-days of our own lives:
school and religious milestones,
birthday hurrahs!

Unfortunately,
there's something about ceremonies
we usually ignore:

They can also be a way to brag:
"Look at us!
See how great we are!"

And we ignore something else.
Ceremonies can have heavy costs—
dollars, time, care—
gifts that could be spent instead
on the have-nots
ravaged by
poverty
and starvation
and war
—the hollow-eyed children
whose world is
fouled and savaged by greed.

*And so we ask ourselves,
"Should we spend our gifts
on celebration
or compassion?*

Or do we spend on both?"
For there is yet one more
justification for ceremonies,
one that is mystic, but strong.

It is the inner, hidden need
to celebrate the glory
of our souls.

For they
are not only eternal
but also merged
with all other souls
and with the creator

—a source of such joy
that we seize on ceremony
to show the world
what this means:
that each of us,
each one,
is embraced by the infinite,
unconditional Love
that makes the universe
sing.

August 17, 2020

Young Black Man
(A True Story)

He is a gifted, personable
young Black man.

Really, he is Brown,
but history has decreed
that he is Black.

So he will always be Black
and he will always
have to be careful
if he wants to avoid
sudden violence
—even sudden death,
because he doesn't ever know
when someone might attack him
just because he is a
Black man.

He is safest if he stays home
which is what he does—
just now.

He plays video games
—sometimes for 24 hours
at a stretch.
That is all he does
except for a part-time
restaurant job.

People all over the world
watch him play video games
because he is
the best.

He didn't always stay home
and play video games.

When he was 13,
his father stood trial
for selling drugs.
He testified for his Black father
at the trial.
He spoke well with dignity,
but afterward,
he got sick
in the men's restroom.

His father asked for a trial
because he was sure
the jury would see he was
    innocent.
But the all-white jury said,
"Guilty!"

Some boys at his junior high
knew his father was
in prison.
They had fun pushing his
"Black prison-father" buttons.

He was an A student,
        good in music,
        good at sports,
but when they
pushed his buttons,
he got angry.

They pushed a lot
and he spent
a lot of time
in the principal's office.

Even so, by the time he
graduated from high school,
he was doing well
again.

But his father came home
just then from prison,
and the young Black man
was ashamed and angry.
This time he stole
$65 worth
of computer equipment
from a store
and he was charged with a
felony.

For the last 40 years
a theft only had to be $300
to be a felony—it was

never increased for inflation.
But lately an even worse law
was created:
"Some retail theft is burglary."

So…
Now he had a
$65 criminal felony record
and he was on probation.

Even so, after a while
the young black man did well
again.

For 4 years he rode his bike
to pre-law college
through ice and blistering sun,
4 miles each way,
4 years of earning A's,
and a magna cum laude degree
in pre-law.

But law school said, "No.
No criminal students wanted."
He could not go on
to graduate school
to become a lawyer.
Not with a $65 felony record.

The only job he could get
was at a restaurant.

So the young Black man
sent in a petition
to erase his $65 felony,
but it languished,
unsigned by the governor
for 4 years,
and then it was denied.

Today his law school hopes
are dead,
and since he is Black,
he still will never know
if someone might
push his buttons again,
or maybe just
shoot him.

So he plays video games
—sometimes for 24 hours
at a stretch.

Day and night he plays,
because then he is
happy.

And people around the world
pay to watch him play
because he is
the best.

February, 2015

Impeachment Manager

Her short hair is grayish blond,
her body thick-set.
Now and then
her glasses slip down her nose
and she pushes them back up
unknowing.

Yet she stands today
a bulwark for democracy
before the United States senate,
speaking of impeachment,
fighting corruption,
speaking fearlessly of
dangers posed by our mesmeric,
compulsively lying and vengeful,
dangerous president.

A lawyer and grandmother
of seventy years,
she stands where, in our beginnings,
women never stood
—being gallery spectators only.
No onlooker, she is
protector of our constitution,
hurling the power
of reason and rule of law
fueled by love of justice,

against the power
of ruthless, cocky ambition
and despotic will
fueled by love of self.

I watch this war of words,
and I am grateful for Zoe Lofgren
and all who fight
to sustain democracy,
to save truth
with its freedom
and its equal rights.

And I worry.
And I hope.

January, 2020

The Lawn

I gaze through my window.
The lawn, clipped smooth,
    stretches to the distant woods
—a miniature park,
cool green and lovely.

        When I mow, the motor's roar
           shatters my senses,
      vines on the fence reach out
           and tangle the wheels.
      Where the grass grows lush
          the motor dies.

The warm breeze carries the sweet scent
    of fresh-cut grass into the house,—
carries the sweet scent of grasses cut today
      and memories of long past grassy sweetness.

        When I mow, dense clouds
          of stinking exhaust
          swirl about,
          choking me.
      A gray trail of fumes
          drifts across the lawn.

The lawn, clipped smooth,
stretches to the distant woods

—a miniature park,
cool green and lovely.

1982

Pandemic
March, 2020

Never before
since the creator said
"Let there be light!"
has this earth seen all its people
driven to cover
—all fleeing
the same terrifying death.

For now the Coronavirus
looms over
every person in the world,
a threat doubly alarming
because we know no way
to stop it.

I look out my window
for reassurance.
The daffodils in my front yard
tell of spring.
The sameness
of my neighbors' homes
comforts me.
But rarely do I see a car pass by
even now in midday.
And strangely,
remarkably,
I see a straggling family of five
going for a walk!

How amazing
that our need for rescue
comes at a time
when the bulging world
can amuse itself
by staring all day
every day
at a cellphone!

—amazing because
that same cell phone
can also bring rescue
to anyone
in danger
anywhere.

And we are endangered.

What if this winnowing scourge
takes from us
all those who create and sustain
our computers
our commerce
our accustomed lives?
Much worse—
what if the Coronavirus kills
those whose wisdom
keeps our democracy alive
—with its equal rights
—its freedom?

But there is hope.

Because this terror
has silenced our world,
we, too, have changed.
In the sudden quiet emptiness
we look about
and see with new eyes.

And seeing the anguish
of those who suffer
and the love shown
by those who risk death
to help the sufferers,
we are flooded
with a sudden need to help,
to strengthen
our inner links to others—
links that stretch
throughout
the world.

Fighting the Coronavirus
April, 2020: Sheltering

Here we are,
fighting a world disaster—
Death by Coronavirus—
and am I volunteering my help?
Not I!
Although my life expectancy
is pretty short at age 91,
to my shame
I'm avoiding the virus with real fear:
staying home alone
gripping safety
with white knuckles.
Helping by staying healthy,
I tell myself.

I do feel some relief
to see that the strangely empty
"sheltering" and "distancing" world
also means for now
a drop in crime
and cleaner air
      that will slow the polar ice melt
now drowning our coastline.

But the world's outer calm misleads.
Hidden turmoil scrambles our minds—
    hospital chaos,
    market chaos,
    family chaos.

And where do I fit in,
in all this chaos?

I experience all dangers by proxy.
I let a friend risk her life
to buy my food;
I let a clerk risk his life
so I can get my meds;
I let a nurse risk her life,
to comfort deaths of others.
Safely separated by television,
I watch a news commentator
broadcast solitary from home—
gasping for breath,
shaking with COVID-19 fever,
fearing death,
"social distancing" in his basement
to keep wife and children safe.

So what am I?
A protected sparrow,
chirping!

We are not ready for this!
Where is God? some ask.

But we are not God's puppets
to be manipulated and rescued.
We are free-standing individuals
here to test ourselves
against the challenges of earth.

Instead of rescue
God has given us
not only our minds
and freedom to choose
but also and especially
our souls
—our inner connection
to each other
and to our creator.

Each of us is unique—
completely in command
of our own response
to this chaos.

We are free to choose
—or not choose—
to accept the challenge of
God's unconditional love for all
as our guide
through this danger
—a gift of freedom that is
proof
of our creator's love
for us.

And proof, indeed,
of his
infinite wisdom.

April 14, 2020

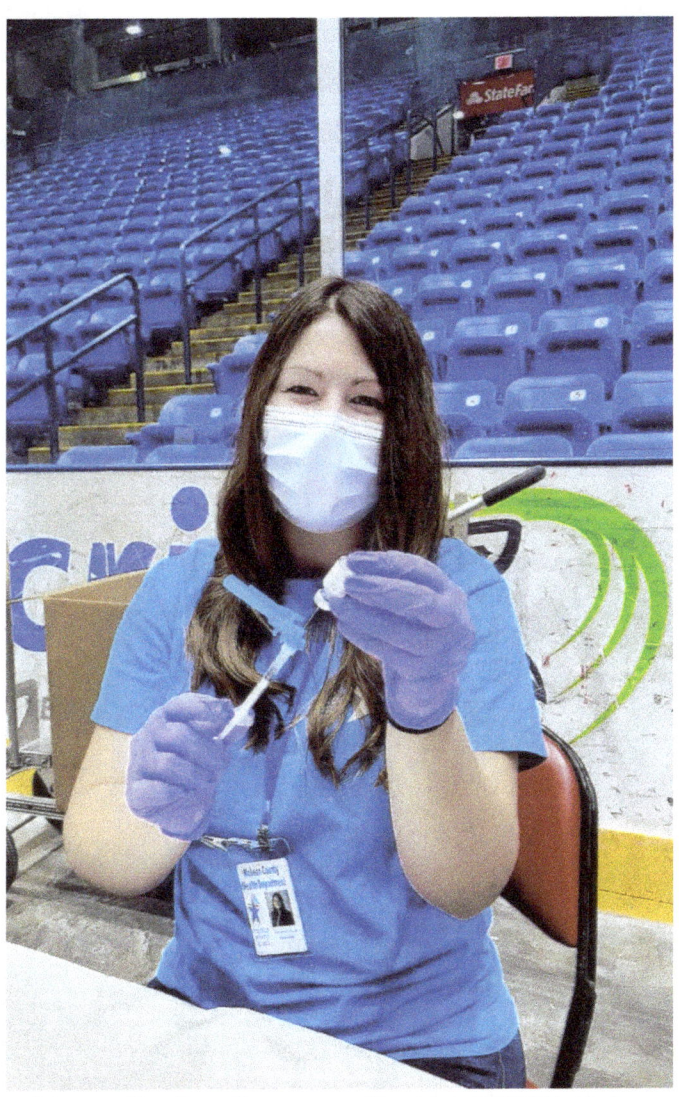
My granddaughter, Shannon, ready to give a COVID-19 shot

Pandemic List
September, 2020

On the Post-It Note by my TV.
I write the daily number
of Americans
who are new
Coronavirus victims.
The total, up to today:
6,611,000.
The death toll:
180,000. *

We see these millions
only as numbers—
unknown, remote.
But a glimpse of lives
behind the numbers
shakes us.
And when we watch
our parents or our children
endure prolonged torment
and die,
these numbers become
unbearable.

This virus is so erratic,
some who are ill seem well,
while those who suffer
for weeks and survive

flounder for words
to convey the agony
they've endured,
the panic of being
unable to breathe.

And, healthy or not,
all suffer because of
the clever greedy ones
who pounce
on the chances at wealth
exposed by this catastrophe,
and hug their foul winnings
with remorseless joy
while the rest of us
watch helplessly
as businesses fail,
jobs vanish,
families are evicted
and schooling is eviscerated—
children
actually begin kindergarten
at home on-line!

But gradually, those of us
who have yet to be "listed"
grow accustomed
to random danger.
Our fear of tortured death
retreats

to the back of our minds,
where it remains.

And very gradually,
we submit, grumbling,
to a mask-wearing,
hand-washing,
distancing
every-day life.

Also, **not** so gradually,
the dreadful list grows.

Some of us,
strangely aloof behind masks
and enigmatic eyes,
begin to use
our new sense of isolation
as a time to wonder
about death—
perhaps to become attuned
at last
to the whispering
of our better angels.

*June, 2022, American deaths:
1,000,000

The Plum Tree in Spring

Gracefully bending
the plum tree stands,
holding clusters of white
        in its slender dark hands.

Then soft winds
brush its brief beauty away
and fragile, sweet petals
        touch earth and decay.

            1959

Time to Get Up

The alarm wakes me.
It's time to get up
and go to work.
Work is a queasy illness.

I'll get up in five minutes.
The bed is a warm womb.
I'll stay in it forever.

Five minutes pass.
The alarm yells.
I emerge with a wail,
newborn,
unwilling.

Barbara Findley Stuart, 1982
State Farm Insurance employee

Summertime Cat

There's fur on the cat.
There's fur in the air.
There's fur on the furniture, too.

There's fur on the floor.
There's fur in the food.
And there's tons of it all over you!

1979

My kittens: Fitz, Peter, and Penny

A Kitten's Tail

I watched our tiger kitten
whirl round and round chasing her tail.
Her white paws pounced
and pinned the furry tail down hard
       for it was a long, writhing
       dangerous beast

Her small needle teeth nibbled at the
nervous black tip whipping back and forth
       for it was a succulent mouse
       trying to escape

Her pink, brush-topped tongue
damply combed the tail's hairs
into shining rows of order.
       It was a tiny kitten all her own
       and it needed washing.

Now she was tired.

She stacked up her white paws
and curved her soft body around them.

She tucked in her furry white chin
and squinted shut her jeweled eyes.

Then her tail crept over the furry paws
and covered her brown nose
      for it was a comforter,
        weightlessly warm.

                1959

If You Should Smile

Do I exist for you?
Am I alive,
you who are here beside me?

Why then when I touch your cheek
do you not touch mine?
Where is the pressure of your hand
when mine is pressing?
Have I no substance
that you withdraw yourself?

Perhaps there are razor fears
or frozen secrets
you dare not touch.

My seeking thoughts
shear away from discovery.
I return to shelter
in the folds of my despair.

Oh, if I should by your response
exist for you.

If you should say
"I see you."

If you should
smile.

1967

Difficult Doors

I need a handyman.
The hook on my screen door
won't latch—
doesn't quite
reach the ring.

But maybe if I
pull it tighter…
and see!
the hook falls into the ring
of itself!

The little door
to the cupboard in my desk
sticks.
It won't open.
It's in crooked

—too tight
against the top.

But I find
that if I press down hard
on the handle
as I pull,
it opens easily.

Sometimes
a search for the cause
and some thoughtful
tinkering
will find an answer—
with difficult doors
as with difficult people
and life
and eternity.

April 2, 2020

Hidden Fire

A fire grows inside the wall,
moving from room to room,
unnoticed
for a long time.

Suddenly it bursts into the open,
roaring out of control,
destroying the home.

A mushrooming fire
of fear and hate
is burning in our schools,
unnoticed
except by alarmed teachers.

A little Black second grade girl
in our neighborhood school
sobs over and over,
shoulders shaking,
"Trump hates me!
Trump hates me!"

Throughout America
small migrant children,
fearing separation,
cry and tremble at school.*

Older children
expand their bullying,
aping their idol,
quoting his insults,
hurling them at each other.
White high school students
at basketball games
chant
"Donald, build that wall!
Donald, build that wall!"
demoralizing their
Latino opponents

The builder of the fire
boasts,
"I just keep pushing
and pushing
and pushing
to get what I want."

He pushes
with whatever bullying
fits the moment—
        lies,
        insults,
threats—
anything to build his fire.

But the fires of hate and fear
will not stay hidden

in these children
forever.
A day will come when
we will cry out
"Where did all this
terrible violence
come from?"

Long ago America
faced down a bullying senator.**
Is there no one today
who will stand and cry out
"Have you no
decency,
sir?"

*Southern Poverty Law Center
**U.S. Army Counsel Joseph Welch

2017

Fourth of July Fears

When I was a small child,
the fireworks at the park
terrified me.
I so dreaded the next flash-bomb
I blocked
even the magic showers of color—
eyes squinted shut
hands a vise on my ears
frozen…
waiting…

I even suffered panic
from the fear
that I would be swallowed up
by the fireworks crowd—
lost forever.

And from dawn past dark,
the random firecrackers
thrown with carefree abandon
by boisterous boys
threatened pain, scars, and death—
with an ear-splitting, shocking
bang!

I cried and trembled all day.

But time taught me
to relax
and free myself from fear.
So now I love fireworks
and crowds of people.

What a gift,
to be so created
that I can learn new ways—
that I can change!

                    April, 2007

Metcalf kindergarten Halloween
Dave and his baseball glove

Halloween Courage

Yesterday
I ran across
an old black and white photo
of my son sitting on the floor
at the front of a dozen other
four-year-old pre-schoolers,
proudly posing
in Halloween dress-up—
    mini-Supermen,
    and tiny princesses.

But not my boy!

No disguise for him.
Just a baseball glove
on his hand.

Pretending to be someone else
worried him.
Only reality felt safe.

On Halloween night
when children,
    electric with excitement
    in the bustling dark,
would ring our door bell,
I would call out,
"Trick-or-treaters!"

He would peer around
the dining room door
at the fantastic visitors
and beat a hasty retreat
to the known security
of our back hall.
I wondered then
if he thought that
once they vanished
inside costumes and masks
children were magically
transformed
into something terrifying,
    something unpredictable.

But perhaps
he simply feared
the thing he did not know.

I thought he was wise
to fear the unknown,
    the unreal,
and courageous
to show his fear
and insist on reality.

I too fear
the unknown—
something new I must try,
something

that might be dangerous,
something evil behind a smile.

Whenever that happens,
I want to have enough
of my son's innocent wisdom
to recognize my fear
and enough of his courage
to hold out for something
that is real
and true.

October, 2005

In Your Beginning

In your beginning
your mom and your dad,
two separate people,
loved
and made a tiny cell
that would become you.
It was hidden in your mom
and only God knew.
But that was your beginning.

You were separate
but connected.

Soon your mom knew about you
and in a few months
you had your soul.
Now you were your complete self,
separate, but connected.
Still, no one could see you.

When you were born
your mom and your dad
could see you at last.
They held you in their arms.
They were full of wonder.
They were happy.
No words could say it.

And they said,
We love you.
We will take care of you
always.

You are yourself.
You are separate.

But you are connected to us
and your soul is connected
to everyone
and to God.

You are your own person,
but when you laugh,
we laugh;
and when you cry,
we cry.

We will love you
always.

October, 2011

Forgiving Dylann Roof

He was a very pale
twenty-one-year-old white youth named
Dylann Roof,
and he dropped in one day
    to join a meticulously-planned
    Bible-study meeting
    at a Black church in Charleston,
silently listening as they pondered
Jesus' parable about sowing grain,
a story saying that some of us
follow Jesus' example
but some of us don't.

These Black Christians
had accepted Dylann as a welcome—
if astonishing—guest,
when suddenly, unbelievably,
deafening gunshots filled the room.
He was shooting one after another
in remorseless rage,
killing nine loving Black people,
targets of his racist hatred,
men and women assembled to find
light to shine on their hardships—
    past slavery
    and present racism,
finding illumination

in their Bible studies—
    love for God, for self,
    for neighbors,
    for enemies.

And the light did shine,
for the survivors said
to their attacker,
    "I forgive you."
One saw only Dylann's ruined life,
    telling him she hoped
    to help him find
    the unconditional love of God
    some day.

But Dylann was deaf to love,
fearing all Blacks as evil,
seeing himself a shining knight
rescuing the white race.

His mass murder,
like their Bible-lesson plans,
had been meticulously planned.
On the internet
he had posted a photo of himself
draped in a Confederate battle flag—
    today's symbol of
    white supremacy—
and posted a diatribe of hatred,
    echoing the mindless rants

of fellow racists,
all blindly unwilling
or unable
to accept
"Love your neighbor.
Love your enemy."

Today, members
of Mother Emanuel church
still search
the teachings of Jesus.
Two years older,
Dylann Roof still sees himself
as America's brave champion
of white supremacy.

Perhaps
these Black survivors
will yet be able to touch him
with their forgiveness,
to reach him at last
with their
unconditional love.

It has happened,
although rarely,
to others.

May, 2017

Sometimes

Sometimes
without warning,
my mind becomes still
and suffused with
a shimmering awareness,
and suddenly
I almost know…

and I think,
If I can only hold on
for just a minute more
and try…

But as soon as I try,
as soon as I even notice,
there is nothing,
and I am empty.

Come again, I whisper,
come again, I say,

so I can know.

1955

My brother Paul and I talk politics

Memorial

Ninety-five
and with a weak heart,
my brother leaned forward intently,
his thin face focused on me,
ignoring the stump of
his right leg.

He said,
"I asked my former assistant
to speak about Islam
at my memorial
and he said 'yes!'
How about that!"
He was pleased
and clearly surprised.

He was sitting in his wheel chair
in the nursing home
planning his funeral.

His recent amputation
did not interest him
—just another
random inconvenience
of old age.
What did interest him was
planning his memorial service.

"I spent years
on peace for the Middle East
and recognizing
the peaceful intent
of American Muslims.
This will be
one more chance
to bring it to people's attention."

Two hours before,
as he was being released
from the hospital,
the nurse had asked him,
"Do you want your jacket?"
His son had answered for him:
"Of course!
and his tie, too
—always!"

Then,
completely dressed
and congressional
in his wheel chair,
he had beamed on us.
"This calls for a photograph!"
He was happy
to look like himself again.
He's still a congressman
at heart
with nation and world

on his mind,
still accepting the inevitable
as he has always accepted it
—a time when he saw war
on a Pacific island,
a time when he ate
chicken heads and feet
for Chinese diplomacy,
and then three days ago
a time when he lost his leg.

Now, looking at
unavoidable death,
he's turning even that
to his purpose,
still working toward
universal peace
and understanding.

It's good
to have such an example
for rounding up a life.

I doubt that I could find
a better one.

October 22, 2016

Knowing Their Name

The hospital room is cold,
white-walled, almost forbidding
except for one sign of life—
the chart of names.
Not just my name
but also the names
of my two nurses for the day.

Other nurses come and go, too,
wearing their names
on their uniforms,
dozens of new names in a few days,
all magicians
well-trained to conjure up
my hidden secrets—
the contents of my blood,
the beating of my heart—
bringing me their magic,
comfort,
and a chance
to return to life.

Of course
they're not magicians
but warmly human women and men
who care so much about people
they spend their days and nights

doing exacting,
sometimes repulsive,
sometimes frightening things—
people with families they love,
demands they must meet,
and joys they seek—
a husband,
a degree,
a new home—
each nurse unique,
each with a separate warmth—
some tender, some brisk,
all, kind.
And each with a separate name,
so many names
I can't remember them.

But I know their name.
It is Love.

January 3, 2021

Christmas Morning
On the Painting by Andrew Wyeth

Her pain,
almost by now a beloved friend,
lingers in the shadows.

For some hours in the dark of night
she has been aware of a change
in her worn body,
a change meaning that death,
like Christmas day,
will come soon.

She has not called the nurse.
Somehow,
meeting death alone
on Christmas morning
seems right.

She lies motionless
on the nursing-home bed,
gazing out the window
at the silent darkness,
watching the imperceptible
creeping of light
work its magic
on the snowy lawn
stretching before her.

It comes to her
that death
is the Christmas morning
of the soul,
when the longed-for
joy of knowing
comes at last—
as when children,
electric with anticipation,
lying awake
in the
early morning darkness,
greet the dawn
with shouts of joy
and rush
to gather the Christmas bounty—
gifts until now
shrouded in mystery.

She has long known
it would be thus,
that her soul would be
freed
from the depths of her body
to see face to face
gifts not dreamed of in life—
a light
like no other,
love
beyond imagining.

Now at last
the snowy lawn
is white and beautiful
in the flood
of morning light.

She smiles,
serene in her joy.

Christmas morning
has come.

                                    December, 2016

November Leaves

Even when
I'm dust and bones,
my ghost
will still remember
a rattling rake
and crisp gold leaves
under burnt blue skies
in November.

1954

Amnesia

I've lost
two whole days of my life.
They've been recorded by Time
but my tape player
isn't working.
Both days are gone.
Erased
as if they'd never happened.

But they did happen.
I'm glad not to remember.
I was nauseated.
Very sick
with something called
Positional Vertigo.
Sick five days and nights
—two not remembered.

But the last two, I
remember too well.
The walls whirled so wildly
I couldn't bear to open my eyes.
I lost 12 pounds.
I couldn't stand or walk.

It's strange
to think about my two lost days.

Although I know what happened
it has no reality.
It's as if I'd read it in a book.
It wasn't me.
Only it was!
I'm told I seemed normal
—very sick, but normal.
I even called my friend
and 9-1-1, myself!

How could I know
what I was doing then
and not remember it now?

I was left out of my own crisis
—an empty stage
providing space
for a drama
but without any connection
—a space still empty
when the drama ended.

My brain
is a miracle created by God,
complex far beyond
any other creation.
I would like to know:
How does it manage
to command chaos
and at the same time

remain
completely detached?

And I wonder.
Will my dreadful two days
suddenly return without warning
some day yet to come,
return with sight
and sound
and sensation?

I hope not.

January 21, 2021

Nosebleeds

When I was 70
I got my first nosebleed.
It wouldn't stop.
I had to go
to the emergency room.

I was scared. I worried,
"Am I going to
bleed to death any day now?"

A good cure for fear is action.
So as soon as I got home,
I put nose clamps by my bed
and in my car,
and then I consulted
nutrition wizard Adelle Davis:
Unexplained bleeding
or bruising can mean
a shortage of vitamin C.

Well, I had no time to test this
because I had a meeting
at the state capitol in two hours
and when I opened the car door
to go—
you guessed it!
another nosebleed.

So I grabbed a few C tablets
and headed for Springfield
with fingers crossed and
nose clamped shut.

Luckily it worked.
So I upped my daily vitamin C
and had no more nosebleeds
for twenty whole years.
But then, sleeping pills
seemed to give me nosebleeds!

After all this time, I thought,
"O no. Not again!"
But at least
I knew what to do.
So first thing, I checked out
the long, threatening list
of side effects for sleeping pills.
(I'm an insomnia "addict")
And you guessed it!
high on the list—
nosebleeds.

So I quit sleeping pills
and boosted the C once more.
And it's worked ever since
—so far.

But this time has been different.
I've not been afraid.

In those twenty years
I've gradually been discovering
the very best cure for fear—
besides action.
It's an off-the-wall cure
that has no logical connection.

It's unconditional love.

I'm finding that
learning to imitate God's love
—to care about people
even when they seem
to threaten me—
affects my whole being.

Nosebleeds as death threat
no longer matter.

Unconditional love
is opening me wide and
scraping away my barriers,
and in doing this
is bringing me peace.
And not only peace.
It's bringing me the thing
I needed most—

courage—
the courage to look at death
without fear.

Unconditionally.

March, 2019

Hearing Aid Rescue

O happy day!
Hooray! Hooray!
You found my sound
—my hearing aid!

—not on the counter
or down on the floor
but under the leaves
on the steps
by the door,

and crawling around
in the dirt
on the ground,
seeking a
"pin in a haystack"
—'til found!

Then, penning a note,
and calling on James
sent it off
straight to me,
safe and sound at my door.

A store with a heart,
built on love
served with zest—

Thank you, dear friends.
Garlic Press
is the BEST!

    From grateful me to the
    Garlic Press gift shop.

January 5, 2020

Ruthann mimics Adlai Stevenson when I pick her up at the Bloomington airport

Homecoming

For a week now
my giant sugar maple
has been
making my whole back yard
a bright yellow—
glowing like the sun,
even in the dark.

But one morning
three days ago
I was surprised to see
the tree was miraculously
no longer a mere yellow
but instead a rich gold
—gold made spectacular
by branches almost black—
and then yesterday's rain
deepened gold and black
to vivid intensity.

"How my daughter will
love this,"
I thought.
For tomorrow
she is coming home from Texas,
where there are
no sunshine maples

—since I have grown too old
to travel to her.

I've been keeping
an anxious eye on my maples,
hoping their fragile glory
would last,
and leave at least
a scattering of bright color
for her to see.

But each day
I've seen less and less gold,
more and more black.

Today my hopes are dead,
for the leaves were frozen
last night
and now fall like rain—
so fast,
they're almost gone.

Regardless,
we,
the tree and I,
just as we are,
await with anticipation
her coming.

For Ruthann
November 11, 2017

Gabriel and the magic tree

Shared Happiness

For nearly a year
I've added photographs
to the pack in the white envelope,
where they swelled tight,
hiding the loved faces
and kaleidoscope memories.
But last week I put them
into transparent sleeves
in an album.

Now they can be seen!

That is my year-old great grandson
enchanted by the Christmas tree,
gazing with new eyes
   at its other-world loveliness,
awed by the green tower
of radiant white lights,
reaching out to touch
its impossible ornaments—
   tiny elves,
     silver angels,
   bright red Santas.

Equally enchanted,
   we watch.

This is my college-student grandson
home for the holiday,
leaning with me over a table
   buried under a mosaic
   of half-inch puzzle pieces,
scanning intensely
for certain colors, certain shapes,
now and then pressing one
into place:
"There's the rest of his hat!"
—small shared triumphs
ending in a
"happy snowman" picture
—at last!

Here we have
four of us in a row,
four generations
in a noisy celebration
of mothers and grandmothers
and the toddler
posing together.
The boy's father has the camera
while his grandfather
cavorts in the background,
making all of us laugh.

Yesterday my neighbor and I
turned the pages
of my newly-created photo album,

and her enthusiasm
bathed me
in an overflow of happiness.

Each moment of joy in life—
   each discovery
   each success
   each moment of love—
is precious in itself.

But when others are joined
   in the moment,
the warmth of shared happiness
spreads in widening circles.

                                February 14, 2016

In Touch

Long ago the ringing of our telephone
could assemble a small,
rather furtive
neighborhood meeting.
We had a party line—
one ring for us,
        two for the house to the north,
        and three for the next;
and since all three of us
could always hear all the calls,
the other two were apt to
just ease the receiver off the hook
very cautiously
and listen in.

Of course "Central" could listen in, too,
so she (it was always "she")
knew everything
about everybody.

And we could find anybody anywhere—
strangers, too—
since "Central" knew all the numbers
even long distance.

We really kept in touch!

But soon all that came to an end
with dial phones.
Now we couldn't use "Central' any more,
and nobody
could listen in.
Instead of "Central"
we now had a phone book
where we could find phone numbers
on our own
and dial anybody,
      even new friends,
even strangers.
All we needed was a name.

So we were still in touch
but with smaller scope.
We really missed "listening in!"

These days
everybody carries a cellphone.
We live in each other's pockets!

We talk to family and friends
constantly
whether they are in Baghdad
or the bathroom.
It's as easy as breathing.
We code in a phone number
and from then on
we just punch their name.

But it can be a real hassle
to learn the cellphone number for
casual friends
or new friends.

Worse, it's pretty well impossible
to find numbers
for long-lost friends or strangers.
Names are no help.

All this is because there is
NO CELLPHONE DIRECTORY
  and no possibility of one.

The world of conversation
outside our
secret, exclusive
"cellphone clubs"
has been swallowed
completely out of reach
along with "Central"
and the phone book,
by the black hole
of technology.

I wonder.
Are we really still in touch?
Or are we
losing touch?

September 22, 2016
309-824-4957—in the rapidly-shrinking directory!

Night Rain

Just a while ago
I lay awake and awake,
sweltering in the steamy heat
of summer
and then silently on my bare feet
I stole from my bedroom oven
to the open front door.

Even here the air is muggy and hot,
but beneath me
the stone steps are cool.
A faint breeze stirs the sultry air.
Rays from the street light,
sifting through restless leaves,
fall, pale and shifting,
on my knees.
Sleep-darkened houses
surround me with silence.
The soft whimper of an owl
calls from afar.

Then comes the fat rich fall
of a few drops of rain,
and soon the sound is like
wind in the trees,
the rain falls so thick
into the cracked, dry lips of the earth.

Now the bricks of the street glisten
and the shadows are wet and shiny.
I sniff the cool, damp air,
newly washed and sweet.
"Ah," I sigh.
Rain has come.
At last.

1957

Morning Light

Each morning
when I awake
in my cool, darkened room,
I reach over
and flick my window shade.
In a flash, up it spins,
flooding my room with
the warmth of daylight,
echoing the rich joy
of the first day:
"And God said,
'Let there be light!'
And there WAS light."
               Genesis 1:3

What a wonder is daylight,
especially when
the sun
streams through my window,
creating prism rainbows
and sunny paths
across my bed
and over my walls.

Every day
I get to imitate God.
Where there was darkness
I can bring light!
I, myself!

However I might manage it,
this is indeed
a gift beyond price.

July 27, 2020

An ice crust for the Fell Avenue bell tower trees

Crystal Moment

The trees awoke at dawn today
to find themselves enclosed in glass
    —each limb, each tiny twig.

They stood about
beneath the white-washed sky
    in icy, mute astonishment
    to be so changed.

I, too, awoke one day to find
a silvery film brushed on my skin
    and whiteness
threaded through my hair.
It's come," I thought, amazed.
"Old age."

For trees, this will not last.
Their crystal sheath will vanish
and tomorrow they will not recall
    their ice-encrusted day—
though coming years
will visit them with crystal
many times.

But I have marked my silvered change.
I know that it will last,
    and coming years
    will see the whiteness grow.

And unlike the trees,
I will recall the morning
I awoke
to know
my crystal moment.

January 31, 2002

My blue-veined hands pulling out all old photos

Old Hands

When my skin grew old and thin,
the veins
on the backs of my hands
bulged blue-black and huge and ugly.

Just like my father's, I remembered.

"I could throw a syringe across the room
and draw blood!" laughed my doctor.

For a long time, it bothered me
to look at them.
Which was constantly.

It bothered me most
when I taught piano.

There were those veins.
Unavoidable.

In front of my eyes
and in front of the eyes
of my young students.

I would say,
"This is what happens
when your skin gets really old.

It gets very thin."

We would both regard my hands.

But at least it had been said
and we could go on.

And I found, after a long time,
that the reality
of my hands
pushed the bulging ugliness
out of my mind.

After all,
when I looked at new music,
my hands and fingers
still knew the places to go,
    the shapes,
        the distances.

After hundreds of exact repetitions
my fingers
would, as usual,
know the intricate patterns
    so well
I no longer had to think
    to direct each action.

In this way my hands and fingers
freed my mind

           to simply understand
           and feel—
free to guide these hands and fingers
through the rise and fall
of the long threads of music
           to seek what was right
           and true
           and strong
           and beautiful.

To seek what was
in the beginning
created by God.

And that is all
in the end
that really
matters.

                    March 13, 2009

Suncatcher

It is very early.
My bedroom is cold, dark and lonely;
not even a cat to rub me with purrs
any more.

But soon the morning sun
floods the glass prisms in my window
spreading its white light
into dozens of sunny rainbows
that shift on my walls
and cascade across my bedcovers.

I catch a rainbow
in the palm of my hand
and play with the bright colors,
making my cold room warm.

Yesterday,
in the sterile operating room
my husband laid his
swollen diabetic foot
before the surgeon's deft hands,
enduring pain,
hoping to avoid amputation.

Soon after,
in his barren nursing home room

nurses exclaimed in disbelief,
shocked at the blood—
the depth of the wound in his heel.

Struck by his need,
his white-haired helplessness,
knowing his bright personality,
his genuine interest in their lives,
they gave him
their comfort,
their skill,
their compassionate love—
making his cold room
warm.

September, 2014

Becoming Deaf

We were sitting on the porch swing,
my brother and I,
watching our reunion family
play croquet.
Our mother, aged 88,
      a crack croquet player herself
      in her Gibson Girl days,
watched too from her lawn chair.
Well—she more listened than watched
since she had lately become
legally blind,
      her vision impeded
      by a macular latticework.

Thinking of her
my brother turned to me and asked
"In your old age
if you had to choose one or the other
which would you rather be,
blind or deaf?"

"Oh, blind!" I said,
thinking of deafness that was total,
and knowing how well Mom coped
with blindness that was partial,
      using audio books and
      writing frames.
I had no doubts.

"Really!" He was shocked. "Not me!
I can't think of anything worse than
never again seeing faces or sunsets,
> never again reading books
> or driving a car
> or playing croquet!
If I was deaf I could still do
all that."

"Well, of course" I argued,
"It would be awful.
But when you're blind
people overflow with sympathy
And the thing is
you can still talk to them

"Not so with deafness,
even partial.
Forget easy conversation.
And forget sympathy.
People are annoyed
when you don't understand them
and they have to repeat—
> especially when you
> **still** don't understand!
And of course
they burst into laughter
when your guesses
are hilarious mistakes.

"However, I must admit
I'd choose deafness, too,
as long as it's just partial.
Being an annoyance and comic relief
isn't that bad.

"But I was thinking total deafness.
I don't think I could stand that.
I'd be too old to learn signing.
I'd be just a watcher of silent movies
without captions
—worst of all,
    never again able
    to talk with my son,
    my daughter,
    my grandchildren.

"Of course I could write notes....

"No.
Even if I had to choose
between totals,
it would be total blindness,
    hard as that would be
—because I would still have a voice
in the lives
of those I love."

For a moment neither of us spoke.
Then my brother nodded slowly,

"Yes," he said.
"Yes.
I see."

Ironically, at 95 he is nearly blind and I at 88 am partially—irritatingly—deaf!

November Light

A while ago I went out
into the cool November afternoon
—already too dark,
too soon.

I was about to turn on the yard light
when I became aware
that no light was needed.
The newly golden maple trees
hovering above me
were glowing
like giant benevolent ghosts,
filling the air
with the magic golden light
of their luminous leaves.

And filling the air, too,
with a fragile rustling—
saying goodbye, perhaps—
for tomorrow
their golden light would be gone.
Tomorrow,
they would be left naked
—black silhouettes
against the sky.
But within their barren darkness
new life would be hiding,

waiting
to dress their black limbs
in green again—

waiting
until the time would come
once more
in the cool dark of fall
when they would again
light the world
for a few miraculous days
with their luminous
golden leaves.

November 5, 2018

Cool Moon

A cool moon rode the sky,
a moon so full of light
it could not hold it all
but spilled light into the midnight sky

and showered whiteness down
through the still, black trees
into the pores of the earth
until the earth
came to life a little
and showed a pale glimmer
of its daylight color.

Silence stretched far off
into the distance
so that tiny sounds were heard.

And God walked the earth
in the white silence,
carrying the moon
in his lustrous hand.

1956

Transformation

Snow edges into my world.
Tiny glass chips
glint in my headlights
and dance and dazzle
and confuse my driving.

The snowy air glows
with smothered moonlight
pink-tinted by city lights.

As I reach my driveway,
swirling snow
whips past my car window,
slapping my face when I exit.

All night
heavy snow batters our house.

With daylight,
turbulent gusts
hurl snow at my neighborhood,
making ghostly trees and houses
disappear,
reappear,
disappear.
At last the snowstorm dies.
Known colors, shapes

have vanished.
The world is transformed.

Clothed in white disguise,
trees and houses are lost
in a wasteland
of snow-dunes and valleys.

Beneath the deep, deep snow
the din of the city is stilled.

Standing silent at my window,
I too am transformed—
stirred by the drama,
the purity,
the miracle.

January 2, 1999

Epiphany

Just now I happened
to hold my hand up
before my eyes,
seeing the palm anew,
moving the fingers,
aware of the bone within,
and suddenly aware
of the amazing confluence
of life-giving nerves,
tissues,
electricity
—sensing
with a rush
the vastness of this universe,
this fantastic creation
with unconditional love
coursing through it,
each living soul awash
in the fierce beauty
of the teeming earth,
each creature
unique
—all richly connected.

And now remembering
John Adams
in his quiet old age
like me,
looking, not at his palm
but at a page in a book
with its scattered dots,
its commas and periods,
and thinking
of the uncounted stars
and sinking into
worshipful wonder
at the mystery
the unfathomable,
beautiful mystery
of this life.

February 2, 2020

Slam-Dunk

I missed the wastebasket.

Balancing
on one bare foot
with supreme concentration,
I held my breath,
spread out my big toe,
pinched a corner
of the crumpled paper,
lifted it,
and this time
dropped it in.

A slam-dunk!
Exultant cheers!

"Use your head
to save your feet,"
my mother often remarked.

Good advice.

Actually, I used them both.
I used not only my head
but also my feet,
this time to save my back
—my arthritic,
90-year-old
back.

It was one of life's
small but satisfying
triumphs.

Pleased and proud,
I sent a brief nod of thanks
to the creator
for his/her provident
ingenuity.

March 7, 2019

Gifts of the Earth

Two days ago,
my back yard was carpeted thick
with sunny yellow maple leaves
the size of my hand.

Then yesterday I raked them to the curb
leaving only green behind,
for winter was coming
and it was time to clean the yard.

But winter was not "coming,"
it was here!
That same day a cold rain
turned into fat, wet snowflakes
and soon the lush green grass
had a light smear of mushy white
and the white snow became so deep
no green was visible.

But there was yet another change.
The few remaining leaves
      —now freeze-killed
—dropped from the trees like rain,
speckling the white expanse with gold.

And so across three days
my back yard has been

    a warm yellow,
            then a cool green,
                        and now a frigid white
                                  with yellow dots!
All this delight
from just a change in the weather.

II

But in those same three days,
a change of weather
on the other side of the earth
        brought agony,
        not delight.

A monster typhoon destroyed
thousands of helpless people.
A towering wall of water
engulfed villages—whole cities
leaving behind only anguish
—bodies of loved parents,
loved children
—unbearably exposed
or buried in stinking mud and rubble,
now a gray land weeping rain.

III

Why, we ask, would God, who is love,
create an earth that

showers us with random delights
one moment
and terrifies us with random destruction
the next?

The answer shocks:
It is because his love for us
is so great
   —so great he turns our souls loose
on this spinning miracle
to stand solitary
except for the bond of love—
to be individuals,
to be independent,
        —not puppets.

Just as in love
we free our own children
to gradually find their separate ways,
the creator sets us free.

And in our freedom
we learn the truths of his creation.
We catch our breath with its joys.
We learn empathy from our own pain,
and, wrenchng free from our comforts
      we learn to embrace
      the suffering of others.
As we live life after life
in this whimsical Earth-Laboratory

with its trials,
we fail,
we triumph, over and over,
until at last we become one
with his great love,
his unconditional love.

November, 2013

Creation

Whenever I think of
the creation of the universe
with all its endlessness,
using only invisible atoms
within electricity
to form its
unlimited vastness,
I am always newly amazed
to remember that
even this simple wooden pencil
is made of an
uncounted number
of those atoms,
each
an unimaginably minute
planetary system
with tiny electrons
whirling about its nucleus
as regularly as we circle
our giant sun
—a miniature universe
held between my fingers.

And then I recall with equal wonder
that amid the stars
that prick the dark sky
are unseen

uncounted
other orbiting worlds
like ours
bristling with other people,
other minds.

We know of these miracles
because curious,
obstinate,
scientific minds
have upended again and again
the time-stiffened thinking
of the world
with their discoveries,
and made plain
these truths.

Equal
in their quest for truth
have been the prophets,
the clairvoyants,
who have experienced
alarming
but ineffable moments
of intense connection
with the hidden realities of God
and who have risked life
and acceptance
to tell us.

Final praise belongs to God,
the creator,
the universal consciousness,
the force,
who with immeasurable love
created each soul
unique,
and embedded his powers
into each of us,
into each brain
with its billions
of electrical connections,
so that we, too,
can know
and create.

June 20, 2018

Hubble Space Image

Outer Space: Small Magellanic Cloud
Hubble Space Image: National Geographic,
November, 2007

In wordless awe
we gaze
past the thin, glowing clouds
and blown veils of mist
of other galaxies
into black infinity,
into the beginning,
into the universal mind.

Amid countless sparks
of lesser stars
hot-white giants shine,
triumphant on their starry points,
bright heralds
telling us of other worlds,
of time,
space,
intelligence
beyond our knowing.

In this fantastic image,
this captured outer space
measured now
between our hands,
our genius
looms large.

But the vast endlessness
of our discovery
dwarfs
our measure.

Still we stay
and gaze
launching into the universe
our questing spirit—
seeking knowledge
seeking meaning

seeking the creator.

January 5, 2008

Autumn 1955

A rattling rake
combing crisp brown leaves
from tangled, clutching grass;

rustling, feather-light mounds
of dry leaves
roaring straight up
toward a deep blue sky
through bursting flame
and swirling smoke;

feathery clusters of birds
clattering in excited chorus;

cool air splitting apart
the cobwebs within me;

a trumpeting rush of joy
shaking my veins

—this is Autumn.

October 26, 1955

My sugar maple

Queen of Trees

Against the sky's
royal canopy of blue
the queen of trees,
the sugar maple,
celebrates
her supreme moment,
lifting in triumph
her black arms,
holding aloft
her blazing crown
of golden leaves,
while the fallen gold
lies spread about her feet—
a regal throne
befitting
her brief splendor.

And we,
her mesmerized subjects,
gaze
and gaze.

Enslaved.

November 5, 2018

A Mystery

Today the maple's dark brown branches
hold only a scattering of golden leaves,
but below
the gold is spread so thick
I forget it's green beneath.

The few remaining leaves
float motionless in the still air,
set off by the dark behind them
like gold medallions on African skin.

A breeze stirs the air.
Now each leaf is a flirt,
bounding lightly on its slender branch,
waving, fluttering, showing off:
"Look at me! How beautiful I am!"

The breeze dies.
Once more the leaves are motionless.

Then, for no reason,
pushed by an unseen hand,
one leaf lets go.

In a solitary dance
it loops and falls in exotic swings,
proudly separate,
flaunting its beauty.

And then it vanishes,
one golden leaf
absorbed into the rich tapestry
of a thousand muted shades
of gold, orange, red—
lost and invisible on the ground,
but still unique, separate.

Among the countless leaves,
whether on the tree
or falling
or resting on soft grass,
each is a mystery of opposites—
outward separateness in
shape, color, and beauty
but at the same time
having a hidden connection
to tree, earth, and air.

I am that leaf
but more intricately created.
I, too, am a mystery,
a finite, unique human being
but at the same time
having a hidden
but eternally and universally-connected
inner self,
also unique.
Call it my subconscious.
Call it my soul.

Although I understand it as little
as the leaf understands its inner link
to other leaves, the tree, the earth,
I feel that my soul—
the real "me"—
provides a connecting link somehow,
mysteriously,
to all souls—
family members
prisoners
tortured children
—all
and in all of time.

And especially I feel
that my soul,
even though I am unaware,
is always connected
to the loving creator
of leaves, people, the universe
—tightly connected
whether I am part of life,
or falling,
or resting.

November 7, 2013

Sweetgum

Last year in the cold of November
the sweetgum leaves
were killed by frost while still green.

Of course, any tree, any leaf
—and any year, too—
has its own pattern of change,
like each of us.

But some years the killing frost is early.
It doesn't harm the bright maples,
but it kills the sweetgum leaves
before they have a chance
to change to red and gold.

The dead leaves hang limp,
dull green and ugly.
Soon there's a steady, softly rattling rain
of dead leaves plummeting to earth
in random order,
leaving at last only a tracery of branches
stretched upward
against the bright sky.

But last year's killing frost
didn't bother my sugar maples.
One frosty day the morning sun

stunned my world
with blinding color.
The trees had turned to gold!
Our house now sat inside a golden bowl
of translucent yellow leaves
glowing in the sunshine
as if the sun had come to earth.

Soon,
like the dead green sweetgum leaves,
these bright maple leaves
began to fall, one after another.
But, quite UNlike dead sweetgum leaves,
these leaves fell joyously,
like yellow butterflies
circling and looping in the sunny air.

Luckily,
my sweetgum got a second chance.
This year was a joy.
The killing frost was so late
the tree had plenty of time
to shake out its harlequin colors
—red, orange, yellow—
sometimes even two colors
on one star-shaped leaf,
colors painted by the sun.
A leaf-point hidden from the sun
under the point of another leaf
would fade to orange

or pale yellow—
or even sometimes remain green;
but where the sunlight touched it
the leaf would burn to a deep red.

How amazing, that each leaf is unique,
and that leaves don't fall all at once,
but in capricious succession,
each at its own time
—like us!

What a bounty of colors,
of change,
of individuality—
none of it an accident,
but springing from the joy and love
of the artist of our universe!

When we see these wonders
that time and separateness and growth
have created with such infinite variety
in trees and leaves
and people,
how can we doubt the plan?
or the planner?

November 11, 2008

The Pin Oak in Winter

It is December
and the pin oak has at last
shed its pointy leaves
to stand bare like other trees.

Well, not quite bare.
Quite a few stubborn
brown leaves
still cling tight,
reluctant to part from
their giant mother.

In brilliant sunshine
against an intense blue sky,
these rebel leaves shine like small
silvery-bronze jewelry,
giving the tree scattered sparkles.
Indeed, it is only pin oak leaves
that reflect sunlight as if metallic.
Even in their summer greenery,
they send out
random diamond flashes.

But pin oaks are messy trees
with frequently falling branches
to gather year-round
and hard acorns that bite bare feet.

And because its leaves fall
late and slowly
we must rake at least twice.

But the squirrels love the acorns.
And I like the sparkly leaves.
So I will try to forgive the pin oak
its sins,
knowing my own frequent need
for forgiveness.

        December 2, 2020

My memory-encrusted Christmas tree

Christmas Lights

I love the lights
of Christmas.

At night
I drive entranced
past a kaleidoscope
of sparkling houses,
each a personal-sized
festival of lights,
each in its own way
banishing the dark
of longer and longer
winter nights.

Inside my house
my Christmas tree,
encrusted with
memory-ornaments and
glowing colored lights,
makes my living room
magical.

But shame creeps in.
I cannot forget
the poverty and homelessness
eating at the world
in other streets,

in ravaged
black cities of war
and sadly, even here.

And yet…
and yet
joy remains.

For Christmas is more than
bright lights
in the December
darkness.

Christmas is
a brilliant searchlight
illuminating
the birth
of indelible words,
words that speak clearly,
luminously
of love,
unconditional,
universal love—
love God,
your neighbor,
yourself,
your enemy.

Because of these words,
love
has become a force
illuminating
the dark world,
especially
at this brief time
each year.

And so
joy
remains.

December, 2005

Colors of the Sun

The sun is bright on my wall
this morning.
And there are the rainbows!
—luminous patches
of red-yellow-green-blue.

Every sunny morning is the same,
for I have hung glass prisms
in each window
to allow for the inching of the sun.

But it was not always so.

At first I had but one small prism
—a sphere, with round-edged facets.
Its rainbows were tiny,
its colors dim to invisible.

Then I found a larger, flatter prism
with broad, sharp-edged facets,
like an out-sized diamond.

Now colors bloomed on my walls.

But soon I noticed that sometimes,
even though the sun was shining
on the prism,

there were no colors at all.
Why? I wondered.
And then I saw.

It was because the prism
had twisted on its string
so that its narrow side faced the sun.
and it could not possibly
bend the light into rainbows.

I gave it half a turn.
Now the broad, jewel-cut side
was square to the light.
Now the colors were again
breathtaking, broad.

"Come, see the rainbows!"
I would cry,
and my children would rush
to see the miracle.

Why is this small thing
so entrancing?
Is it because of the miracle
of sunlight making
    these colors glow
like no other colors
in nature,
or the mystery
of colors emerging

from colorless light,
or the magic of seeing
miniature rainbows
        shimmering on our walls?
It's all these, of course.

And it's the same with people.

Sometimes a rainbow
of warmth and love
is sealed inside people.
But no one else will ever see it
unless the searchlight
of selfless,
unconditional love
of another person
shines on them,
and even then only if they are
turned to catch the love fully.

So, too, it is with God

We cannot know
the shining joy of God
unless we find his light
and turn
so it shines through.

It is only then—if but briefly—
we will know
the colors
of his great love.

March 3, 2013

From my front porch: a fantastic sunset

My family, 2022.
My son Dave and Geri; Zach Kusch; me; Dustin Stuart; Megan Kusch-Carrillo and William; my daughter, Ruthann Kusch and Megan's Gabriel; Shannon Stuart. Dave Kusch had injured his leg and gone home to Texas.

About the Author

Barbara Findley Stuart, a wife, mother of two, grandmother of four, and great-grandmother of two, was born July 11, 1928 in Jacksonville, Illinois.

As a child Barbara loved to ride her tricycle along the sidewalk, often accompanying a passing-by neighbor no farther than the boundary set by her mother, talking all the way. Communication—and books and writing, any way to share her love of people and life—has always come first. As an adult her loves morphed into other kinds of communication. Music was often at the center, especially piano and singing—she sang for weddings, church, and funerals, composed songs and piano music, taught piano and school music—even played the Tchaikovsky piano concerto with the university orchestra. But family, especially her much-loved son and daughter, made the core of her life. And always there were words and people: teaching English, serving as an elected county board representative, writing stories, speeches, and opinion letters, and creating and chairing committees—committees that have worked to strengthen justice and prevent violence and racism.

Then around 80, Barbara became too deaf for committee work or teaching. Fortunately, a good friend introduced her to a small group who also love books and writing. She soon came to value poetry as a bridge past her deafness, emailing her poems to friends and family and taking copies with her everywhere she went—and giving them to friendly people. Then, if her deafness did not keep her from understanding their speech, she would end up in a warm discussion of the poem's ideas.

In her lifetime she planted 61 trees, the last a pink dogwood!

At 94, Barbara is grateful that her poems are helping her make friends in her new life in a retirement home, and is especially happy to now have a poetry book, to reach out to others.

I would like to thank the Publications Unit at Illinois State University and its graduate students Saima Afreen, Emily Fontenot, and Kamryn Freund for working on this book of my collected poems, guided with expertise, patience, and kindness by Steve Halle, Director of the Publications Unit.

7-11-2022

www.ingramcontent.com/pod-product-compliance
Lightning Source LLC
Chambersburg PA
CBHW071737150426
43191CB00010B/1613